# DR ROXLEY FHATUWANI MASEVHE

## Against all odds
### from grass to grace

## by Ndivhuho Thavhana

**Proofreading by Dr Roxley Fhatuwani Masevhe & Aluwani Manenzhe**

**Text Design & Layout by Ndivhuho Thavhana**

**Cover Design by Ndivhuho Thavhana**

**Cover Artwork Advisor: Linken Seloane**

**Venda language advise & guidance: Dr Rasila Naledzani (for some words).**

**Dr Masevhe's website:** https://roxleymasevhe.co.za/

**Email:** info@roxleymasevhe.co.za

**Bishop Masevhe's Cell: +27 72 985 2017**

El Shaddai Graphics - https://elshaddaigraphics.co.za ;
Ndivhuhot@gmail.com

*AUTHORISED BIOGRAPHY OF*

# DR ROXLEY FHATUWANI MASEVHE AGAINST ALL ODDS – FROM GRASS TO GRACE

**BY**

NDIVHUHO THAVHANA

**PUBLISHED BY**

*El Shaddai Graphics*

# PLEASE TAKE NOTE

Words in italic are not English, e.g. *misevhe* (arrows). The English explanation is in brackets (arrows). An example of this usage is: [the following songs: "*Muṅwe na muṅwe u ḓo fhira* [everyone will pass on from this world]".

The Venda word "*Vho*" in front of a person's name is a prefix to show respect just like in English when we use Miss/ Mrs/ Mr, e.g. *vho* Masevhe, in English, it would be something like Mr Masevhe or Mrs Masevhe.

The Venda word "*Ha*" is a prefix used in respect of many places in Venda, e.g. *Ha*-Mutsha, *Ha*-Magidi.

#

**KINDLY TAKE NOTE** that this book is written in a slightly larger font to cater for elderly people who have already given an indication of interest in reading the book. Smaller fonts are not as readable for may elderly people.

# FOREWORD

*"Bishop Masevhe is a servant of God called when he was young, a prince from the Masevhe Royal Family. The things he would say and sing was evidence of his calling.*

*He is not only a pastor, a prophet, apostle or Bishop, but he is also an exceptional leader. He has planted so many churches all over. He takes care of his family. I have joined him in prayer at the mountain on many occasions.*

*I also travelled with him out of the country as he was ministering. I am one of those he prayed for, and my situation was resolved. I say to God: Long live Bishop Masevhe!"*

**MUSANDA, CHIEF RAMULONGO,
HA-RAMULONGO, TSHIVHASE**

*"The first time I saw Bishop Masevhe performing was at a youth camp. I was not born again, but I loved singing.*

*My love for music and the way he performed his music ministry and played the guitar forced me to hang around as I wanted to know more about this man and his music.*

*He composed my first album, and he and Mrs Daphney Masevhe were part of my backing vocals for that album.  I thank him for his encouragement that has bought growth in my music ministry. I say to Doctor R F Masevhe, let the show go on."*

## MRS REJOICE THINA MUKUMELA

*"Bishop Masevhe is a great encourager, and if you are willing, he allows you to showcase your skills.*

*Whilst travelling in the USA I found a JVC Keyboard, the same keyboard model that Bishop Masevhe had. I had never seen it before, but Bishop Masevhe would tell us beautiful stories about that keyboard.*

*I ordered it for him, and when I surprised him with the gift, he was overjoyed. Both of us were crying. The old JVC keyboard was famous. I recall hearing listeners on Phalaphala FM referring to Bishop Masevhe as Roxley Masevhe and his golden keyboard.*

*Had it not been for Bishop Masevhe, where would I be, I wonder?"*

### GABRIEL "THE GREAT" TSHISIKULE, A MUSIC PRODUCER

*"In February of 1982, I was touched and transformed by the song A huna Mulalo kha vha sa tendiho Mudzimu (There is no peace for those who do not believe in God).*

*From then on, I started to attend church at Kutama Pentecostal Holiness Church. On 30 May 1999, I was baptised by Pastor Lorraine Luvhengo.*

*I am thankful for his effort in my life, maybe I would be dead, but now I stand in front of people and preach Jesus Christ with confidence. May God bless Bishop Masevhe.*

*I remember an outstanding performance by Bishop Masevhe at the Mapungubwe Arts Festival in 2008 at Polokwane. Most of the artists who performed before him were miming and playing background music, but when Doctor R F Masevhe ascended the stage he was singing live, and this revived the crowd. I really enjoyed that performance."*

**EVANGELIST TSHIMANGADZO MAEMU**

*"The community was not surprised at how good a singer Bishop Masevhe was since both his parents were exceptionally good in what they were doing.*

*Bishop Masevhe was the choir conductor of all the school choirs: junior, intermediate and senior.*

*It was a spectacle to watch Bishop Masevhe conducting a choir. She states that it was as if he was possessed or drunk and that it was clear that this gift was in his blood."*

**DOCTOR THIDZIAMBI GLADYS ṊETHENGWE, ASSOCIATE PROFESSOR AT UNIVERSITY OF SOUTH AFRICA**

*"It is not possible to read about this life and remain the same. Bishop Masevhe's life will*

*challenge you to persevere, to rise higher and to go on against whatever odds that may come.*

*I remember as a student when Bishop Masevhe came to Dimani Agricultural High School and showed the students a video on "Hell" what one should expect in hell. That memory remains etched in my brain."*

**NDIVHUHO THAVHANA
AUTHOR, LEGAL ADVISOR, GHOST WRITER &
GRAPHIC DESIGNER**

# Dr Roxley Fhatuwani Masevhe, Against all Odds: From Grass to Grace

NDIVHUHO THAVHANA

*Dr Masevhe (he prefers Bishop Masevhe because of his calling as a pastor. Dr is an honorary title) is thankful to the many loyal and loving fans out there who have supported him through thick and thin. It is impossible to name them all, but he is really honoured by the support and love he has received.*

# BIRTH

Roxley Fhaṱuwani Masevhe was born at Thengwe, which is in Thondoni Village (in the former homeland of Venḓa) in the Limpopo Province in South Africa on 24th September 1959.  He was born at the Thengwe Local clinic, and the nurse on duty, the late Mrs Christinah Ravhuanzwo, gave him the name Fhaṱuwani, which means awakened/witty/smart. When he was older, he asked this nurse why she had given him that name. She responded that when he was born, around midday, he was active, energetic, and with a beautiful smile, or should we say, a handsome baby smile on his face, unlike most children at birth.

# EARLY SIGNS OF GIFTS AND TALENTS

Bishop Masevhe was involved in music and dance at an early age. It comes as no surprise as both his parents were actively involved in music. He has heard of how at the age of seven years, he would dance to the rhythm of his mother's wooden spoons' (*lufo* and *lufheṱo*) cooking sounds. She cooked food in a clay pot using wooden spoons. This type of cooking was the typical Venda traditional style of cooking, especially the porridge, and even now, many people still cook this way. These were the early signs of his musical and dance talents.

# FAMILY

**VHAVENDA MUTAHABVU VHO MATHUNTSHA THIRUMIWI RECKSON MASEVHE**

His late father, Vhavenḓa Muṱahabvu (the late) Vho Reckson Mathuntsha Masevhe, was a famous guitarist who played the guitar at parties during the 60s and 70s. Bishop Masevhe's father passed away in 2019.

The Masevhe clan, are chiefs, and have their land at Madzivhanani at Thengwe Village, in the northern part of Limpopo Province in South Africa.

He was a regent on behalf of Victor Nndwamato Masevhe (who was still young by then).

**TSHINAKAHO DZONAKELA MASEVHE (BORN MUKOSI)**

He would go to pray at the mountain whilst he was still at (UAAC) United African Apostolic Church under the late archbishop Miriri.

Bishop Masevhe's mother, Mrs Tshinakaho Dzonakela Masevhe (born Mukosi), was a leader of the traditional Tshigombela Dance Group. Tshigombela is the Vhavenḓa traditional female dance.

The young Bishop Masevhe and his mother accompanied his father for his performances at parties.

According to Doctor Thidziambi Gladys Ṋethengwe (wife to the reigning Chief, the senior traditional Leader *Thovhele Vho* (Mr) Vudzidzhena Ṋethengwe, at Thengwe Village), Mrs Tshinakaho Dzonakela Masevhe was an exceptional dancer. The Tshigombela dance group she was leading was a pilot project (traditional dance project) chosen from the whole of Venda. Doctor Thidziambi Gladys Ṋethengwe was one of the dancers under the leadership of Bishop Masevhe's mother, even though she was a teacher. The dance group was selected as a pilot project when the late Former President of Venda, Chief Minister Patrick Ramaano Mphephu, had visited Tshandama Primary School.

Doctor Thidziambi Gladys Ṋethengwe states that the community was not surprised at how good a singer Bishop Masevhe was since both his parents were exceptionally good in what they were doing.

His father, being a traditional chief, married four wives, following the Vhavenda custom for traditional leaders (chiefs).

His father's first wife, Martha (*Marita*) Masevhe gave birth to Tshilidzi (the firstborn of Bishop Masevhe's father) Nthambeleni and Joyce Masevhe.

Mrs Tshinakaho Dzonakela Masevhe was the 2nd wife to Bishop Masevhe's father. Bishop Masevhe is the firstborn son of his mother and the second born to his father. He has three (3) siblings: Calvin Takalani, Thivhavhudzi Rollet and Ṅaledzani Desmond Masevhe. He has no sister from his mother's side.

Mrs Modiane Claudina Mopipi is the third wife, and her daughter's name is Mmathaphelo Masevhe.

The fourth wife, whose name is was *Vho* Nyadzanga, had one son by the name of Emmanuel and is late.

His father's brother's name is Jack Masevhe and was born of the same mother (Thangammbi) as Vhavenḓa Muṱahabvu (the late) Vho Reckson Mathuntsha Masevhe.

# ORIGIN OF THE SURNAME MASEVHE

The surname arose from the word misevhe (arrows). According to Bishop Masevhe's father, their forefathers used poisoned (*vhutulu*) arrows a lot in fighting with their enemies so much that they were great warriors and were awarded land in Madzivhanani Village. The Masevhes originate from Masvingo in Zimbabwe and have also settled in Homba on a mountain which they own. As hunters, the Masevhe's lived near borders as they sometimes crossed the borders to hunt. They did this in Zambia, Botswana, Maleboho and Venda.

# ABJECT POVERTY

Bishop Masevhe's family lived in abject poverty. His father was a labourer at Dzimauli General Dealer and then went to work as a farm labourer at Doreen Citrus Farm (known as *Dolina* farm). When he left Doreen Citrus Farm, he went to work as a migrant worker in Johannesburg, Gauteng Province (more than 600km away from home) as an assistant in the carpentry business.  By this time he was not yet the regent, he became a regent towards the end of his life.

Bishop Masevhe's mother tilled the fields. The family would wake up early, around three in the morning to go and till the ground. They preferred working in the early hours of the day as Thengwe is very hot and humid during the day. Around six in the morning, Bishop Masevhe and his siblings would then prepare to go to school.

The family was so poor that their best meal on Christmas Day or Good Friday was bread. They would buy the bread from Maṱatshe (travelling on a donkey cart about 60km) about three or four days before Christmas Day. They would then dry the bread to prevent it from becoming stale. They could not afford to buy bread or meat more often.  The stable meal was vegetables and porridge. Once in a blue moon, the family would slaughter one of the chickens at home for a proper meal.

Bishop Masevhe would hunt birds at the mountain.

*He spent most of his youth barefooted. Shoes were a luxury he and his siblings could only dream of having one day. He picked up his first shoe from a dustbin in Musina and sewed them together with a wire.*

He remembers that they were brown in colour.

Bishop Masevhe remembers that at some stage of his school life, he only had two pairs of trousers. He had to wash one trouser each day to make sure he had a clean pair of pants to put on the following day.

# LADZANI PRIMARY SCHOOL

Bishop Masevhe attended school at Ladzani Primary School in Thengwe Village.

Doctor Thidziambi Gladys Ṋethengwe was a teacher at this school during the time that Bishop Masevhe was a student. She recalls that the school choir won several times at the eisteddfod competitions. Bishop Masevhe was the choir conductor of all the school choirs: junior, intermediate and senior. According to her, most of the teachers at the school were also good choir conductors after the training they received from teacher Philemon Ndanduleni Maudu and the late Mr Ramagoma.

Doctor Thidziambi Gladys Ṋethengwe says it was a spectacle to watch Bishop Masevhe conducting a choir. She states that it was as if he was possessed or drunk and that it was clear that this gift was in his blood.

She described him as a brilliant student. She recalls one incident when the late principal Mr Mavhungu Ḓivhambele-Maano Felix stated: "The Masevhe children are intelligent, but when it comes to Fhaṱuwani, he is by far the most intelligent of them all." It was during the meeting on whether or not to promote him to the next class. The school promoted him from Standard B (now known as Grade two) to Standard two (now known as Grade four).

A teacher caught Bishop Masevhe sleeping in class on the first day of school when he was then in Standard one (1). This was before the class levels were referred to as grades. When the teacher inquired, Bishop Masevhe explained to the teacher that the Mathematics the teacher was teaching them was boring him as he already knew the contents of the prescribed book for that year. Principal Ḓivhambele-Maano Mavhungu, testing Bishop Masevhe, opened the very last page of the book and asked him to do calculations there. Bishop Masevhe was able to do the calculations efficiently and correctly. That is how the school principal promoted him from Standard 1 to Standard 2.

He excelled in poetry and was the number one poet from Sub A up to Standard 6 level of that time.

Bishop Masevhe still remembers that the name of the Afrikaans poem was "*Muskiete-jag*".

He obtained a first-class in the then certificated Standard 5.

His brother, Doctor Ndivhaleni Masevhe (son of Jack Masevhe, the brother to Bishop Masevhe's father), confirmed that Bishop Masevhe had a photographic memory. He recalled how he excelled in commercial subjects and would obtain 100% for some of his tests.

***Bishop Masevhe formed ROFMA [Roxley Fhaṱuwani Masevhe Evangelical Music Ministry] when he was still a student.***

The aim was to spread the word of God using music. He met Simon Neḓohe, now Professor Doctor Neḓohe, who was playing the concertina/piano accordion (gorostina) then (Lostlake Music, 2020).

He also met Itani Madima, now a pastor, Michael Ṱhavhana (now a pastor), after he had finished studying at Rhema Bible School]. He also met Mr Kenny Mathivha, now Limpopo Premier's Spokesperson. Pastor Goodwin Ramazhamba, Nthumeni Ḽigamela (now pastor Ḽigamela), a pentecostal pastor, Pastor Edward Phaṱhela [mushavhi (of Jewish descent)], Pastor Ratshiṱanga, (now Bishop Doctor Ratshitanga), Mr Point Nephawe, Simon Munyai, the two Nemurangoni brothers, Patrick Mahani, Hendrick Khangale, Thomas Maphophe, now a leader in the Assemblies of God, the late Bishop Joseph Makwakwa, Maurice Chauke,

Prophet Hlungwani (who had a church in Giyani) and many others. They teamed up under ROFMA to spread the word of God all over Venda, especially the villages.

Through ROFMA, Bishop Masevhe met Doctor Tshifhiwa Samson (TS) Muligwe of Rhema Kingdom Life Centre, with whom he travelled in ministry the longest.

Doctor Tshifhiwa Samson (TS) Muligwe of Rhema Kingdom Life Centre teamed with ROFMA. They launched the following Baptist churches: Folovhoḓwe, Muswodi, Tshipise, Mukovha wa Bale, Thengwe, Sambanḓou, Dzimauli, Mianzwi and Dzingahe.

Doctor Jonas Ntshavheni Bvumbi [spiritual son of priest (*Tshifhe*) Ḽivhebe, (fondly referred to as *Tshifhe* Ḽivhebe) hosted a crusade at Thengwe Village to spread the word of God. Bishop Masevhe was both a worshipper, playing the guitar and the assistant pastor for this team.

Bishop Masevhe was put in charge of Thengwe Baptist Church. The following people were born again at this church: Pastor Ṋemuṱanzhela (a junior traditional chief), received Jesus Christ during the crusades with Doctor Tshifhiwa Samson (TS) Muligwe. Other pastors who repented whilst Doctor Tshifhiwa Samson (TS) Muligwe and Doctor Jonas Ntshavheni Bvumbi were preaching were: Pastor Takalani Rathogwa. Pastor Mudzweḓa, Pastor Godfrey Ṋenzhelele, Pastor Mbedzi and Pastor Nonani Xivambu.

Bishop Masevhe continued under ROFMA and ministered in many villages: Ngweṋani, Tshiḽapfeṋe, Muwaweni Ha-Mulima, Tiyani, Magoro. He held many youth conferences.

# PERSISTENT POVERTY

Despite excelling in school and being so good in music and dance, poverty forced him out of school. Bishop Masevhe went to work in Musina, a town, about one hundred and ten (110) kilometres away from Thengwe Village. Bishop Masevhe borrowed two rands (R2.00) for taxi fare. A white man, an Afrikaner nicknamed *"Tladi"* (a Sotho name meaning thunder lightning), employed Bishop Masevhe to work on his farm. As well as his Fruit Shop which was in town.

There was a day that year in 1974 when Bishop Masevhe arrived late for work at the fruit shop in town. He had to walk from the *Tladi's* farm to the shop in town, and the farm was quite a distance from town. *Tladi* gave him a thorough beating with a folded electric kettle power cord and put him inside cold storage for a long time. Inside the cold storage, Bishop Masevhe agonised in pain and prayed to God to save him. By then, he was already a prayerful person. *Tladi* later took Bishop Masevhe out of the cold storage room at the fruit shop and drove him back to the farm. *Tladi* was cruel. He used his car from the farm to town, leaving his workers behind to walk the trip on foot, and when they were late, he would be outraged. This was normal for most farmers then. Bishop Masevhe ran away to work for another farmer.

This farmer was a racist. One day the farmer's sons gave Bishop Masevhe some tea to drink.

***As he drank the tea, he realized there was urine inside, and that the boys were making fun of him saying, "bobbejaan, kaffir!" (bobbejaan is Afrikaans word for baboon, "kaffir" is nigger in Afrikaans). That was one humiliating experience for Bishop Masevhe, one he will never forget***.

On this same farm, Bishop Masevhe was required to sweep the yard, and because it was Autumn the leaves kept falling from the tree all day long, and the farmer told Bishop Masevhe to clean again, until there was no leaf left, meaning he spent most part of the day sweeping.

Whilst he was working in Musina, Bishop Masevhe could not afford to rent accommodation and had no place to sleep. His uncle Peter Mukosi (brother to his late mother), who was working in the mine, would sneak him into the miners' compound at night. This was during the apartheid regime, and by then, it was illegal for a black person to be loitering around town, either during the day or the night, so Bishop Masevhe had to avoid arrest.

When the police would come to search the compounds, Bishop Masevhe would hide behind the uncle as he was thin on a cement bunker. At times, the uncle would sneak him out of the room, and Bishop Masevhe would hide in the water pipe until the police left. If it was raining, he had to make sure that the water in the pipeline did not sweep him away.

In the mornings, the workers would be fed *ndengane* (*lambaza*) soft porridge which cooked in big open pots, and it was common knowledge that at times cats would fall into the *ndengane* (*lambaza*) soft porridge and it would still be given to the workers to eat. They had no choice but to eat the because of lack of money to buy food.

At that time, there used to be a drive-in cinema in Musina and only whites were allowed to watch the movies but the black people, as always, made a plan to bypass this racist restriction. They would climb the trees and watch the film from there. The only movie that blacks were allowed to view was a bioscope called *"Penga"* who was a thief. Lever Brothers would play this to blacks as they were promoting soaps: *ḓambavhakegulu* (a long bar soap, quite smelly, with an ugly colour and made specifically for black people), Sunlight, Lifebuoy, Omo and Surf.

At work, Bishop Masevhe earned four (R4, 00) rands per month. He used two rands to buy shoes (not new), a pair of trousers and a shirt and the other two rands as bus fare to go back home.

It was difficult for Bishop Masevhe's father, who was in Gauteng, to send money back home.

When Bishop Masevhe went back home, he still wanted to attend school. He came up with a brilliant plan, and approached one of the local businessmen, Mr Andries Makhitha Ṋeswiswa, a wealthy man, and requested him to allow him to look after his cattle in return for the man sending him to school. Fortunately for Bishop Masevhe, the man agreed. Mr Neswiswa employed Bishop Masevhe to work at his restaurant and butchery in Thengwe Village.

One day, Bishop Masevhe woke up early so he could take the cattle for dipping and still make it to school on time. It was a freezing day. The thorns called Devil's thorn 1 (*museṱo* in Venda) and the Amaranthus spinosus (Mabogo, 2012) (commonly known as *tshithavhamisisi*) were piercing his legs. Because his legs were frozen, he could not feel the pain. Only later, when it became warmer, and his legs started to swell did he realise he was severely injured. Such were the odds that he had to endure.

# JUGGLING

He juggled the life of schooling in the morning and herding cattle in the afternoons for a long time.

At times he would cut tall grass used for roof thatching of rondavels for different people to make income.

---

1 Family name: Pedaliaceae. Botanical Name: Dicerocaryum zanguebarium (Lour.) Merr. Museto (Venda), Devil's thorn (English). (M.P. Tshisikhawe, 2019).

As boys, Bishop Masevhe and others would also fetch the logs for the roof. They would carry them on their shoulders in bundles. The roof repairing was an annual routine.

Despite all these activities, to survive, he still needed to help his mother in carrying the mealies from the field to bring them home. They carried them on their heads using traditional basket, *mithathe* and *zwirundu* (traditional hand-made (woven) baskets).

Mr Ṋeswiswa would drive Bishop Masevhe, Thifhinduli Phalanndwa and Tshidimela Phalanndwa (older brother to Thifhinduli) to where his cattle were and leave them there to herd the cattle back to Tshandama in Thengwe.

Some of the routes were about one hundred to one hundred and ten (100 -110) kilometres away from Thengwe. Places like Mbodi, Maṱaṱani, Tshamuṱavha, Maremanzhi, Ḓambale, Domboni (Ṋiani area).

When the cows were too tired to walk, the boys would bite their tails to force them to walk.

***One scorching day, while herding cattle in the field, Bishop Masevhe became so thirsty he ended up drinking the dirty water the cows were drinking.***

They had to herd the cattle through the harsh forests, and by then, the trips were long as they had to go around the farm fences. There were no shortcuts.

The boys would camp overnight in Shakadza Village and spent the night with relatives of Mr Makhitha.

On another day Bishop Masevhe lost cattle in the bushes. When Bishop Masevhe found them, they were amongst other cattle, and unfortunately for Bishop Masevhe, all these cattle had the same reddish colour, and he was confused, not knowing which cow belonged to his employer. Bishop Masevhe cried to God, in prayer, for help in identifying his employer's cattle, and God was faithful and helped him identify the right cows.

On another day Bishop Masevhe and friends were herding a big whitish ox. The owner, Mr Andries Makhitha Neswiswa, had told the boys that if anything happened to that ox, he would kill them. During the evening, while herding it back home, the ox fell over a cliff and fell on top of trees, and they being so scared, ran away thinking it was dead. Bishop Masevhe spent that night in prayer, asking God to intervene and save the ox.

The following day Bishop Masevhe went back to the veld and found the big whitish ox (called Afrikaner and in Venda, many people call it *frukaner*) grazing and healthy. He spent that day ululating, dancing, singing and thanking God that the ox was alive. He did not want to be killed for an ox. As Bishop Masevhe was busy dancing, people came out of their rondavels to check if he was going crazy or not. They found out that he was celebrating the fact that he was not going to be killed.

Another source of income was herding donkeys.

The fact that Bishop Masevhe's family was too poor to afford candles or paraffin for study lamps in the evenings did not deter Bishop Masevhe.

*He would use either the light from the firewood or moonlight or when they money for paraffin, tshikenzekenze (home-made paraffin lamp made from a glass bottle (or can) to hold the paraffin and a piece of fabric as the burning rope).*

Bishop Masevhe would carry porridge and Wild Jute 2 (also referred to as bush okra[3] or (*delele*)) to school as his lunch break meal.  His family could not afford to give him pocket money.

Bishop Masevhe remembers how he would walk from Thengwe Thondoni Village to Thengwe High School, a distance of around forty (40) kilometres. Despite the daily long walks to and from school, Bishop Masevhe performed well at high school. He achieved a first-class for the then form 3.

In grade 12 he qualified to study for a bachelor's degree. By this time he would study during the week and perform at conferences and crusades over the weekends. Despite the hard life, Bishop Masevhe saw God in his life. He succeeded against all the odds.

---

2 Family name: Tiliaceae, Botanical name: Corchorus tridens L.    Delele (Venda), Wild jute (English) (M.P.Tshisikhawe, 2019).

3 (The tribe, 2020) refers to "*delele*" (scientific name: *corchorus olitorius*).  Called "bush okra" in English].

# PROLIFIC DANCER

As Bishop Masevhe grew up, he also joined (UAAC) United African Apostolic Church and excelled in the dance music known as Zion *maḓembe* music (*maḓembe* means miracles). He excelled in playing the drums and dancing at UAAC that he had no competition worthy of note. He was the champion dancer.

He was an excellent *malende* dancer (*malende* is traditional Venda dance) as well. He danced *malende* during the ancestral worship ritual sessions when his family on his grandmother's side was appeasing the gods. As the firstborn, he would beat the big drum to the gods, and his younger brothers played the smaller drums. At that time, they could not see the difference between worshipping gods and worshipping God in heaven.

As he grew up, he evolved from loving the *malende* dance to *Mbaqanga* [4]. Bishop Masevhe excelled in *Mbaqanga* dance and earned the nickname diesel "dizili" (just like a diesel engine that endures longer) Bishop Masevhe could go on and on for long hours dancing without getting exhausted. He was dancing to *Mbaqanga* music, amongst others, the music of Mahlathini and the Mahotella Queens, and others.

---

4 [ (Wikipedia, 2020) defines **Mbaqanga** as (Zulu pronunciation: [mbaˈǃáːŋa]) is a style of South African music with rural <u>Zulu</u> roots that continues to influence musicians worldwide today. The style originated in the early 1960s)].

# BOYHOOD

Bishop Masevhe and his brothers would herd goats in the veld. During festive season celebrations, the brothers were forced to stay in the bushes, looking after the goats, while others would be celebrating and putting on new clothes.

*Bishop Masevhe grew up loving bird hunting, either with the traditional wooden slingshot (commonly referred to as lekere by Vhavenda people) or with vhulimbo (a sticky bird trap made by chewing the barks of a Mukwatule tree that traps the bird on contact). Once a bird was caught in the trap, he would rush up the tree, forgetting that he might fall.*

Bishop Masevhe and Mushoni Magome (son to his mother's elder sister whose name is Nyaluḓangani) would sneak away during school time to go bird hunting. During one of their sneak aways, Bishop Masevhe fell from a very high tree while looking for bird's eggs in a nest. Mushoni thought Bishop Masevhe was dead, so he ran away to go and get help, but when he looked back, he realised that Bishop Masevhe had lifted his head. Bishop Masevhe had dislocated both his legs and had to crawl back home. Doctor Thidziambi Gladys Ṋethengwe would instruct other boys to run after them to stop them from dodging shool. It was only one boy, Lovhi Mapengo, who could catch the fast Bishop Masevhe as he was also a fast runner.

Bishop Masevhe loved hunting and eating grasshoppers, *ṱhonono* (crickets), *nzenene* [5] (bush cricket (Wikipedia, the free encyclopedia, 2020)). This is a delicacy for many people.  He also loved the flying insects, called *mabembenene.* You find *mabembenene* (these flying insects) on tree leaves and you can either catch them or hit them with a stick as they require considerable skill to catch. If you are not careful, they fly away. Bishop Masevhe would run very fast after the flying *bembenene,* and catch it, and this confirmed his nickname "Diesel." Bishop Masevhe states that according to doctors, *Mabembenene* insects are full of proteins.

Bishop Masevhe and his brothers also enjoyed catching fish. One of the fun times for Bishop Masevhe and his friends was hunting for bees, and as boys, they would compete.

***As boys, it was such a privilege to be bitten by bees. It was a symbol of being "man enough".***

One day Mbambadzeni Luṱingo Masevhe once brought expired honey from the mountain. This was not ordinary honey but is known as *Done* honey, (the insects producing this honey are much smaller than bees). Mbabadzeni Luṱingo Masevhe is an elder brother to Doctor Ndivhaleni Masevhe from the same father, Jack Masevhe. He is an elder brother to Bishop Masevhe. The boys ate the honey and became so <u>drunk.</u>

5 Nsenene is the Luganda name for Ruspolia differens: a bush cricket (a.k.a. katydids or misnamed "long-horned grasshoppers") in the tribe Copiphorini of the 'cone-head' subfamily.

Usually, if the honey is not eaten within a certain period, it expires and must then be cooked first; otherwise, it makes a person drunk, and it makes one bite their tongue. To prevent injury, people put sticks in the mouth of the intoxicated person. That time, the elderly ladies asked Bishop Masevhe what he had eaten and when he described what hey had eaten, they knew that it was this type of honey and quickly gave the boys unripe fruits mixed with breastmilk to induce vomiting. They made soup out of the breastmilk, and the chopped fruits.

***At some stage, Doctor Ndivhaleni fainted, and his mother was crying, thinking that he was dead.***

Bishop Masevhe prayed out loud  "I have faith in God that he will not die". The elderly ladies then force-fed him with breastmilk, and ultimately he woke up.

Bishop Masevhe is ever thankful to God for his life and that of these boys. As we speak, Ndivhaleni is now a Doctor, and Bishop Masevhe is also a Doctor and multi-award-winning artist showing that God had planned good things for these lives.

\#

As a young boy, Bishop Masevhe, would collect empty food cans, sit under a tree, and use them as drums.

Bishop Masevhe was also good in making music by blowing air through a semi clenched fist (referred to in Venda as *tshipoṱolio*).

He also played *"Madumbukalinga"* (a jazz guitar like a makeshift, one-stringed guitar.).

Doctor Ndivhaleni Masevhe confirmed that Bishop Masevhe was an intelligent young man.

Doctor Ndivhaleni Masevhe remembers the exercise books brand name, Croxley that students used in school.

***Bishop Masevhe erased the "C" from the word Croxley and come up with the word "Roxley", and hence he is still using the name Roxley.***

Bishop Masevhe had an aunt by the name of Evelyn Sieda, wife to Bishop Sieda, who was a prophet. Bishop Masevhe wished to be a prophet, and with time the spirit of prophecy started to manifest in him, and he became one of the prophets prophesying like her. She was a prayerful woman who would go to the mountain to pray.

In those early years, Ladzani Primary School hosted a church crusade by Pastor Lawrence Ṋemukula of the Presbyterian Church.

***Pastor Lawrence Ṋemukula preached a powerful message, which transformed Bishop Masevhe. Bishop Masevhe admits that this***

*message brought repentance into his heart. This was in the early 70s.*

Unfortunately, one of Bishop Masevhe's friends spoke vulgar words against the pastor. Bishop Masevhe tried to rebuke the friend, who was older than him, but the friend told him to shut up. Since he knew his friend was a bully, Bishop Masevhe kept quiet for fear of a beating. He asked his friend: "Why do you speak against a man of God as he is preaching the word of God and not his message?"

In the evening, after the church crusade, Bishop Masevhe and friends headed home walking along a narrow path in the grass. They walked past a particular spot and then some moments later, heard one of the boys shout from behind, "Snake, snake". They ran back only to find out that it was the same friend who had spoken vulgar words against Pastor Lawrence Ṋemukula. A red snake had bitten him.

*From that day on, Bishop Masevhe started to fear God. He became convinced that you should not speak ill of the servants of God.*

As a young boy, Bishop Masevhe loved music so much that his dream was to one day be a well-renowned musician. When famous artists would perform in Makwarela Location at Mutsila Hall, Bishop Masevhe would attend the all-night music festivals. The trip from Thengwe to Sibasa by bus was about one rand fifty cents (R1.50) or two rands (R2.00) by then (currently in 2020, it is R25.00).

After the festival, he would sleep over somewhere in Makwarela and head back home in the morning. Bishop Masevhe remembers performances by the group Harare and other artists like Sipho "Hot sticks" Mabuse, Maurice Mukwevho (well known for being an excellent bass guitarist in Limpopo) who performed with Irene Mawela and The Mahotella Queens.

One of the famous artists by then was late Dziedzi Maphiri, would perform at Thengwe High School, and Bishop Masevhe was more than happy to pay the entrance fee to watch this artist's performance as he admired the artist.

# HOMEMADE GUITAR

*In 1977 Bishop Masevhe made a home guitar using an old square fish oil tin (can) and fishing rod strings as guitar strings (tshiṱurumbadza/tshibenzhi).*

He carved the fretboard (fingerboard) from wood. According to his brother, Doctor Ndivhaleni Masevhe, Bishop Masevhe's guitar turned out to be a nuisance at times, as he would play the guitar at all hours, including at night when the other family members were sleeping or wanted to sleep. Nevertheless, they endured the nuisance, not aware that this was the beginning of great things to come.

Sometime later, Bishop Masevhe carved another wooden guitar from *muvhale* tree (common coral tree [6]). People told Bishop Masevhe that he should be careful as he will go crazy. By then, when one played the guitar, people believed it would lead to madness.

# THE GIFT OF A GUITAR

Nevertheless, he excelled in playing this makeshift guitar. People started to recognise his talent. He was still at UAAC.

*The first proper guitar that Bishop Masevhe owned was a gift from one of his friends, Kennedy Sitsula, who is now an advocate (counsel).*

He was a student at Tshivhase Secondary School. By then, Kenneth Sitsula, Nthumeni Ligamela (now a Pastor), Ailwei Shavhani, and Siṱhari were staying in Vhufuli, the village next to Donald Fraser Hospital. This group would attend church conferences organised by Doctor Lennox Ṋemukula, the younger brother to Lawrence Ṋemukula at the local Presbyterian Church at Maḓonoro in Vhufuli Village, next to Donald Fraser Hospital.

A white man, a Christian doctor, had given this guitar to Kennedy Sitsula. Kennedy Sitsula worked as a gardener for this doctor. Fortunately for Bishop Masevhe, Kennedy Sitsula decided to hand the gift

---

6 Erythrina lysistemon Hutch.Family: Fabaceae. Common names: common

coral tree, lucky bean tree (E), gewone koraalboom, kanniedood (A), umsintsi (X), muvhale (V), mophete (Tsw), mokhungwane (Sotho), umsinsi (Z) Fabaceae/ Leguminosae (Pea & bean family). (SA National Biodiversity Institute, n.d.).

over to Bishop Masevhe as Kennedy knew nothing about playing the guitar.

Bishop Masevhe woke up early to travel to where Kennedy Sitsula was, to pick up the guitar. He walked through the bushes and forests from Vhufuli through Makhuvha, Ḓamani, Makonde, through the farms, past Mutale, crossing Nyahalwe river through Tshishivhe Village, and then to Thengwe (about forty-five (45km)) through the forests. Bishop Masevhe was so excited to receive his first acoustic guitar. By the time he arrived home, it was late at night as it had been a long journey. Within a week, he had taught himself how to play the acoustic guitar. It was the year 1977.

***As a student, Bishop Masevhe would take his guitar to school. During break times he would play the guitar.*** The students would gather around him to watch the young Fhatuwani as he showcased his skills. The teachers rebuked him on many occasions, to no avail but because he was a hard worker, he still performed well in school attaining first class during the final exams.

***Bishop Masevhe received Jesus Christ as Lord and Saviour in the year 1977 during a revival by the late Reinhard Bonnke***[7] in Venda at Makwarela Location Stadium upon invitation by the late Doctor Maswole Ragima.

---

7  Reinhard Bonnke (19 April 1940 – 7 December 2019) was a German-American Pentecostal[1] evangelist, principally known for his gospel missions throughout Africa. Bonnke had been an evangelist and missionary in Africa since 1967. (Wikipedia, the free encyclopedia, 2020).

***Tommy Saiden, who was the crusade worship leader of Reinhard Bonnke's ministries, Inspired Bishop Masevhe to become an instrumentalist.***

Bishop Masevhe loved his style of worship. Pastor Kenneth Meshoe (now Reverend Meshoe) and Pastor Konisang from Lesotho were some of this crusade leaders.

After the revival, the late Doctor Maswole Ragimana arranged for the baptism of those who had become born-again at Mvuḓi River. So many people wanted to get baptised he had to ask his assistant, *mushavhi* Pastor "Kulu" Sadiki (*mushavhi* meaning he is of Jewish descent", to help. Bishop Masevhe is one of those who were baptised that day.

In 1977 the late Doctor Maswole Ragimana was a Faith Mission church Pastor. By that time, the church met for fellowship in a house before relocating to a school classroom.

On the day of the baptism, bishop Masevhe travelled with others in a truck, all the way from Rambuḓa Dzimauli, under Bishop Ramulifho "the *dunamis*". It was through Doctor Maswole Ragimana that Bishop Masevhe and others came to honestly know and understand about the baptism of fire and speaking in tongues. The late Doctor Maswole Ragimana's church was well known for miracles. People referred to it as *maḓembeni* (the home/place of miracles). By then, the late Doctor Maswole Ragimana was still holding services at Gindikindi Primary School in Makwarela Location.

Bishop Masevhe acknowledges that it was under Bishop Ramulifho "the *dunamis*" that he, personally, really came to know the Lord as His Lord and Saviour, not just a matter of saying "I receive Jesus Christ as my Lord and Saviour". The church fellowshipped at Dzimauli Village, at Rambuḓa and they would hold their baptisms at Faith Mission Church at Makwarela Location.

**In 1978, Bishop Masevhe composed several songs using the guitar that Kennedy Sitsula had given to him.**

One of the songs he composed was titled "*Vhudzisani makhulu vha ḓo ni vhudza*" [translated to English it means "ask granny, he/she will tell you"]. The other song titled "*Thothotho [8] I khou fhedza vhathu Venda*" in English it means "home-brewed beer is killing people in Venda". *Thothotho* is a local home-brewed beer that was poisoning a lot of people in Venda at that time.

The other song was "*Mutuku na delele a si u ḓifha*". "*Mutuku* (sour porridge) n*a delele* (Wild jute[9], also referred to as bush okra[10]) *a si u ḓifha* (so tasty)"

---

8 Botswana takes the gold in naming its backyard brews. It has tho-tho-tho, (the dizzy spell), a lala fa (you sleep right here), laela mmago (say goodbye to your mother) chechisa (hurry up) and motse o teng godimo (there is home in heaven). (Mutunga, 2010).

9 Family name: Tiliaceae, Botanical name: Corchorus tridens L.      Delele (Venda), Wild jute (English) (M.P.Tshisikhawe, 2019).

10 (The tribe, 2020) refers to "*delele*" (scientific name: *corchorus olitorius*).  Called "bush okra" in English].

meaning "sour porridge with *delele* (Wild Jute/ bush okra) is so tasty".

*Mutuku* (sour porridge) and *delele* (slimy green vegetable) meal is a Venda delicacy. Bishop Masevhe himself is a lover of this delicacy. *"Tshiambela tshi nukha sa mushidzhi* (Blackjack)[11] *wa Makonde"* meaning "Rude language smells like Blackjack vegetable found in Makonde." He was composing songs out of compassion for the community to teach them about life. In this instance, he was cautioning people who were dying from drinking home-brewed beer to stop drinking.

# RADIO VENDA BROADCASTING STATION

Radio Venda Broadcasting Station loved his early songs, like *"Poṱilo hangala"* (Venda folklore songs). In 1978, the station recorded some of his songs and aired them, and this made Bishop Masevhe big and famous.  This was his first recording. Munaka "Stinka" Ramunenyiwa recorded and produced these songs.

---

11 Family:Asteraceae. Botanical name:Bidens pilosa L. Mushidzhi (Venda), Blackjack (Engish). (M.P.Tshisikhawe, 2019).

# RADIO ṰHOHOYANḒOU BROADCASTING STATION

Radio Ṱhohoyanḓou Broadcasting Station, started operating in 1979 in Ṱhohoyanḓou in Venda. The station recorded the following songs: *"Muṅwe na muṅwe u ḓo fhira* [everyone will pass on from this world]", *"Dakalo* [joy]". Mr Mudau from Radio Thohoyandou is the one who recorded Bishop Masevhe.  Bishop Masevhe became a household name gospel superstar in the whole of Limpopo Province, then known as Northern Transvaal. He was the top gospel music recording icon.

Another album he recorded in 1979 was *Vho* Maria also recorded by the then Radio Venda.

*Doctor Tshifhiwa Samson (TS) Muligwe used to hold church camps at Gondeni ḽa Mabilu Village, and Bishop Masevhe was one of the regular attendees. The camps, titled Youth for Christ, were held during the school holidays around June and July, and these camps brought Bishop Masevhe closer to Jesus Christ.*

Some of the youth camps with Doctor Tshifhiwa Samson (TS) Muligwe were co-organised with the help of Pastor Lennox Nemukula and his then co-worker in ministry Khuliso Nemadzivhanani (who later became the registrar of the University of Venda).

The messages preached at these camps were relevant to the youth of that day.

*Bishop Masevhe recalls Pastor Maḽori Mavhetha of Nazarene Church, at Folovhoḓwe, who would allow him to preach at his church. A fantastic opportunity for the young Bishop Masevhe.*

Bishop Masevhe would visit places like Gogobole with another trainee pastor (being trained under the Nazarene Church), Pastor Rakhadani, (a good friend of Bishop Masevhe) and Amon Alidzuli.

During his conferences at Khubvi Village, the late Pastor Makhari employed a lot of Bishop Masevhe's services. Bishop Masevhe ministered through music using his guitar.

Bishop Masevhe also travelled with the late Pastor Lawrence Takalani, a great servant of the Lord from whom Bishop Masevhe learned a lot of things.

Bishop Masevhe was one of the artists who performed at Ṱhohoyanḓou Stadium during the 1979 Venda Independence celebrations. Venda was celebrating their independence from the apartheid regime. The stadium was full, and Bishop Masevhe was given a chance to perform and sang the song *"Muṅwe na muṅwe u ḓo fhira* [everyone will pass from this world].

*The masses loved the song, but the chiefs (mahosi) present were not impressed with the irony in the song and ordered the security personnel to instruct the sound engineer to mute the microphone to abort his performance.*

Bishop Masevhe was furious. After this sabotage, he approached Dean Tshenuwani Farisani to complain, who responded to him: "There is no way, these leaders will love you. They have joined the Boers (Afrikaners) in oppressing our people, and you are telling them in public that they will pass from this world and will not enter heaven."

After the day's event, Bishop Masevhe would sleep inside the freezing tent, with his jacket and shoes on as he did not have enough money to travel to and from home for the next day's events. The jacket and shoes did not help as his feet would freeze.

*Bishop Masevhe is the first person in Venḓa to sing gospel music whilst playing musical instruments and is regarded by many as the Pioneer of gospel music in Limpopo.*

As far as Bishop Masevhe can remember, the other person who played music with instruments at that time was (*Moruti*) Pastor Ndlovu in the then Eastern Transvaal Region. (Moruti) Pastor Ndlovu played the guitar, and people would throw money into the round hole of his acoustic guitar. This was in the year 1979.

Around 1980 Bishop Masevhe performed (his first wedding performance) as an artist at the wedding ceremony of Bishop Doctor Ramulifho, the *dunamis*.

He was still attending school. The wedding was well attended. Bishop Masevhe recounted how he felt the anointing of playing the guitar and singing fall upon him so strongly on that day. After the wedding, the host gave Bishop Masevhe a formal suit as he did not have decent clothing.

It was the same year (1980) that Radio Venda recorded his album, *Vho* (Mr) Piet.

***In 1981, Doctor VS Ramasuvha and his wife invited Bishop Masevhe to perform at their 10th wedding anniversary celebrations at Venda Sun Hotel*** (now known as Khoroni Hotel Casino Convention Resort[12]). It was such an honour for this hungry village boy to perform at the grand hotel before the well-to-do celebrities of that day.

After the performance, when Doctor Ramasuvha wanted to pay Bishop Masevhe, Bishop Masevhe negotiated with the doctor to help him with his school tuition fees.

Bishop Masevhe performed at many weddings: amongst others, the wedding of Mr Kutama, Dr Chris Rabali and Julia Nthakheni at Rabali Village in Nzhelele. It was before people started capturing weddings on video cameras. By then people used still photograph cameras only.

He passed his form 3 with a first-class in 1979.

---

12 Khoroni Hotel. (Resort, n.d.)

*He was forced to break from school due to a shortage of funds. He opted to become a private teacher (known then as temporary teaching). For the year, 1980, he worked as a temporary teacher at Mufulwi Primary College, with two other teachers.*

For Bishop Masevhe, it was by God's intervention that he was employed at the school. He approached the principal, who without any hassles, told him to come and report for work. As this was happening, he recalled Psalm 77, which says God is a miracle worker who has manifested himself unto the nations.

*Bishop Masevhe started to see God's power manifesting in his life, more so, after he received Jesus Christ as his Lord and Saviour.*

One time, the school principal left him alone in charge of the school. There were so many students at that school (Grades A, B, standards 1 and 2) and he instructed the children to go into the bushes to catch grasshoppers. He was keeping them busy to stop them from loitering, and they filled a 12, 5 kilograms (kg) bag.

*It was at this time that he taught "Muafrika" (a sports radio personality who is also a reporter for Kick-off Magazine, a soccer magazine, Mr Edshine Phosa) who was then in Standard 1.*

The first few months of that year, poverty was at its worst as he could not even afford to eat properly. He spent months feasting on these grasshoppers as his food.

Another student he taught is Silas Nduvheni, who is now a journalist with Daily Sun Newspaper.

The other reason why Bishop Masevhe had to work that year was that he wanted to pay school fees for his siblings.

It was the following year, 1981, that Dr Ramasuvha pledged to help Bishop Masevhe with tuition fees. Bishop Masevhe then went back to school. He was still juggling between being a student and music performances.

Bishop Masevhe also performed at the wedding of Pastor Silas Nefefe as well as the wedding of Samuel Makhado at Gogogo.

He was in Standard  11. It was this year that he memorised the whole Economics book. His Economics teacher, Mr P Ravhuanzwo, can confirm this.

# POVERTY GALORE

Bishop Masevhe was still using the light from the wood fire and the moon to study. There was still no money for paraffin. That year (1981), he performed well academically and qualified to study for a bachelor, but unfortunately for him, there was no money to pay for his tertiary studies.

Because of poverty, the family would burn sugar in a teaspoon with fire and then throw it into the tea mug, and the water would turn brownish mimicking the colour of tea. They would then add regular sugar (not burnt) to sweeten the drink.

Regular food (*tshisevho*) for the family consisted of natural insects like *madzhulu* (Termiterium[13]), *nemeneme* (flying termites[14]), *nthwa* (flying termites) *thonono* (crickets), *nzenene* [15] (bush cricket). Food which Bishop Masevhe enjoyed.

## *He would sew his torn sneakers together with a wire*

The family had no comb and used a wild tree branch (*gwanda*) as a comb. They used the Devil's thorn [16] (*museto* in Venda) as bath soap. For a toothbrush, they used *Mutshevho* tree (Phoenix *reclinata*)[17.] You chew it and then guggle with water afterwards. Bishop Masevhe depended on his grandmother for food, Christmas clothes and other basic necessities in life.

---

13 Termiterium and flying termites (known as madzhulu, nthwa, and nemeneme respectively). (Mabogo, 2012).

14 Termiterium and flying termites (known as madzhulu, nthwa, and nemeneme respectively). (Mabogo, 2012).

15 Nsenene is the Luganda name for Ruspolia differens: a bush cricket (a.k.a. katydids or misnamed "long-horned grasshoppers") in the tribe Copiphorini of the 'cone-head' subfamily. (Wikipedia, the free encyclopedia, 2020).

16 Family name: Pedaliaceae. Botanical Name: Dicerocaryum zanguebarium (Lour.) Merr. Museto (Venda), Devil's thorn (English). (M.P.Tshisikhawe, 2019).

17 ((RSA), 2020).

*The trouser she could afford was called Sendeka, he had to tie it with elastic around the hips. When the elastic became stretched they would use the ties that the old men brought from Gauteng as belt*s.

The shoes they wore then were *tekkies* (sneakers kinda but not even that good) commonly referred to as *mapfutseke*. The shoes were named *mapfutseke* because if someone was giving you the shoes and it was not your size, they would just say *voertsek*[18] (Afrikaans word for "get lost").

The other type of shoe then was *phashane*. It was made out of a car tyre. A person would place their foot on the tyre, and then someone would cut the sole of the shoe out of the tyre to fit your foot size and then slice thin layers from the tyre to serve as the shoe ropes. Some refer to them as Batata Sandals[19].

# ANOTHER GUITAR FINANCED BY FORBE'S SON

After some time, the first guitar (the gift from Mr Sitsula) wore out and had to be replaced. He then received another guitar, his third guitar. Keyboards

18 (Wiktionary, The free dicionary, 2019).

19 (Africa Smiles South Africa, n.d.).

were still not in fashion. Dean Tshenuwani Farisani, dean of the Lutheran Church, organised everything.

*Missionary Forbe's son financed the guitar, all*

**BISHOP MASEVHE WITH HIS FIRST ACOUSTIC GUITAR**

*the way from Germany. By then, Bishop Masevhe used to spend a lot of time at Dean Tshenuwani Farisani's place.*

Bishop Masevhe performed at the wedding of Mr Joseph Rasivhetshela who married Dean Tshenuwani Farisani's sister. Bishop Masevhe also performed at Percy Nemaembeni's wedding and Pastor Boy Mbedzi's (now a doctor, with an honorary doctorate in Theology) wedding.

Bishop Masevhe and Dean Tshenuwani Farisani travelled to Polokwane which is approximately two hundred and forty-one kilometres (241km) from Thengwe to buy the acoustic guitar. The guitar was operated with a PM10 battery and had a galaxy speaker. To the young Bishop Masevhe, this guitar was a miracle. He played this guitar at so many weddings. The famous wedding song then was "Amen, Amen *iyo si zo ngena* "Amen, amen, we will enter."

# LESSONS GALORE

Bishop Masevhe remembers the period he remained behind at Maungani Village, with Dean Tshenuwani Farisani's wife, Vho-Regina (whom he fondly refers to as his mother) and the mother to Dean Tshenuwani Farisani. Dean Tshenuwani Farisani had been arrested for his political involvement during the apartheid era.

Bishop Masevhe recounts how Vho-Regina Farisani taught him to wash the bathtub after bathing. Coming from a poor family, Bishop Masevhe had no idea that after bathing, one had to clean the tub.

Dean Tshenuwani Farisani was in jail, and they had no idea where the police were holding him.

During Dean Tshenuwani Farisani's absence, Bishop Masevhe recalls that strange and mysterious things would happen. Trees would catch fire out of the blue and at some point, a burning tree nearly fell onto the mission house. Lots of snakes would just be found around the house/yard, but they killed them.

Bishop Masevhe remembers Dean Tshenuwani Farisani's mom as an intelligent woman.

Dean Tshenuwani Farisani (Dean of Lutheran Church, Devhula /Lebowa Circuit of ELEXA (Evangelical Lutheran Church of Southern Africa) was arrested with the late Reverend Phosiwa (also of the Lutheran Church in Maungani), the late Reverend Mahamba (also of the Lutheran Church in Maungani), Zwo Nevhuṱalu (spiritual son of Dean Tshenuwani Farisani, the late Rev Mahamba) and Professor Simon Ṋeḓohe.

These were people with whom Bishop Masevhe interacted a lot, and at times they were forced to sleep on trees to avoid arrest by the police.

Bishop Masevhe remembers that when Tshifhiwa Muofhe was murdered, he, Bishop Masevhe was now politically literate as he was spending a lot of time with politicians. He was mingling with people like the late Pastor Lawrence Khorommbi and his wife, the old man, the late Pastor Makhari, and Pastor Lawrence Takalani. He travelled with these servants of God, ministering through music either at conferences, weddings, revivals, crusades and church services.

The old men, the late Pastor Makhari and the late Pastor Takalani, were some of the people who shaped Bishop Masevhe's life. They taught Bishop Masevhe that he must study and make a career for himself to make it in life.

At the time that Bishop Masevhe travelled with the late Pastor Lawrence Khorommbi, he was the leader of ECO, named from BECO (Bold Evangelical Christian Organisation). Some of the worship team members of ECO were the late Mr Livhuwani Mavhina, Khathutshelo Mavhina, the late Dziedzi Maphiri, Thivhavhoni Lidzhade (now a pastor), Itani Madima (now a pastor), Seani Netshisaulu and others. These group exposed him to the fulfilment of the great commission.

Bishop Masevhe travelled around a lot with different pastors at different times for conferences, revivals and church services. He worked a lot with the late Reverend Mahamba, who was also a well-known Venda Author and at some point even stayed with him. He remembers how the Reverend Mahamba would wake them up around three (3) in the morning to pray.

Even though Bishop Masevhe's father worked far from home, God ensured that he sent his servants from all walks of life to train his son, Bishop Masevhe, in the way of the Lord.

# THE GUITAR FROM MR RAMSEY BOY

The second guitar also wore out and had to be replaced. The late Mr Ramsey Boy, a teacher and a fan who loved Bishop Masevhe's music so much, bought a guitar for Bishop Masevhe. Bishop Masevhe also performed at Ramsey Boy's wedding at Tshiozwi,

Madombidzha during the late 80s.

# TAXI DRIVER CONFISCATES HIS BELOVED GUITAR

One day Bishop Masevhe ministered at Gogobole, in the Nazarene Church, with his friends Nelson Rakhaḓani and Pastor Amon Ṅaledzani. Afterwards, Bishop Masevhe boarded a taxi at Louis Trichardt, to go to another church, at *Ha*-Mutsha Village, to minister through music. The taxi driver used the route commonly referred to as Lwamondo *murahu ha thavha* (Lamondo travelling behind the mountain).

In the taxi, Bishop Masevhe was busy playing his guitar, singing the song, *Muṅwe na muṅwe u ḓo fhira kha ḽino shango* — "everyone shall pass from this world". The taxi driver became furious with Bishop Masevhe, accused Bishop Masevhe of mocking him and confiscated the guitar from him. Unfortunately for Bishop Masevhe, he did not have another guitar for his next performance. He prayed and cried unto God, pleading with God. He asked God to ensure that he received his guitar back if indeed, God had truly called him as an artist. By then Bishop Masevhe was staying with Mugivhi family, in *Ha*-Mutsha Village. He became close friends with their daughter, Ndivhuwo, who was a teacher. This family loved God. His friend, Ndivhuho eventually got married to teacher Maṱamela. She loved Bishop Masevhe's music and was a great fan who sponsored the ministry often.

Later on, Bishop Masevhe was informed, that upon arrival at his home, the daughter of the taxi driver (who had taken his guitar) told him "you have taken the guitar from Fhaṱuwani Masevhe, a real child of God". The daughter added that she knew Bishop Masevhe well and described him as a man filled with the Spirit of the Lord. She begged the father to immediately return the guitar to Bishop Masevhe. The taxi driver could not sleep one night with the guitar in his possession.

The taxi driver was forced to look for Bishop Masevhe and eventually left the guitar at *Ha*-Mutsha Village with a Masevhe family, unknown to Bishop Masevhe. The family of the late Mr Samuel Masevhe, who was an Agriculturist (*Mulimisi*) sent out a message to notify Bishop Masevhe that they had his guitar. Bishop Masevhe was informed that the Masevhe Family were looking for him and eventually went to pick up his guitar.

Upon further enquiry, Bishop Masevhe was told that the taxi driver was not able to fall asleep with the guitar in his house.

Bishop Masevhe continued to record other songs.

# AN ARTIST IN DEMAND

After some time, Mr Mudau from Radio Ṱhohoyanḓou Broadcasting Station went to Bishop Masevhe's village to record more of his songs, and this shot his fame even higher. He rose from zero to hero, from ashes to somebody and was now a star.

By the year 1982 Bishop Masevhe was so famous he was performing in most weddings and conferences. He was an artist people sought after.

# FIRST INVITATION TO TRAVEL ON CRUSADES

*Bishop Masevhe remembers that the first people to invite him to travel around on crusades and conferences was evangelist Doctor Tshifhiwa Samson (TS) Muligwe, Apostle Doctor Maxwell Masakona and Doctor Jonas Ntshavheni Bvumbi (Bishop Masevhe fondly refers to them as fathers). This was during the years 1978 -1982.*

The nearer he got to Jesus Christ, the more poverty started to fly out of the window. Poverty started to evaporate, like dew as the sun rises.

Bishop Masevhe also travelled with Pastor Livhebe, the late Pastor Lawrence Khorommbi, and the late Doctor Maswole Ragimana. Amongst them was Pastor Athalia Mavhutha (whom he fondly refers to her as his mother). These servants of God are some of the many who contributed much to his spiritual growth.

Bishop Masevhe has fond memories of how in 1985 he shared a stage with the legendary Yvonne Chaka Chaka, Chicco Twala, William Mthethwa, Om Alec Khaoli and other famous groups of that time at Thohoyandou Stadium. He estimates that the crowd by then could have been around forty-five thousand (45,000.00).

# FORMAL EMPLOYMENT

Bishop Masevhe approached the Deputy Minister of the then Venda Government, Post and Telecommunications at his home highlighting his plight for a job. The minister told him to come to see him at his office. When Bishop Masevhe arrived at the office, the minister hired him.

As a result, from 1983-1986, Bishop Masevhe worked as a private secretary for the Deputy Minister of Post and Telecommunications in the then Venda Homeland Government, Khosi *Vho* BR Nemulodi. *Thovhele* Vho

(Mr) Vudzidzhena N̂ethengwe, at Thengwe Village was the one who recommended that Bishop Masevhe be hired for this job.

In 1984 Bishop Masevhe composed an album for vho Hilda Ratombo, titled *"Zwimangadzo"* (surprises) which was recorded by BK Productions. The favourite song in that album was *"Ri tshi vhona zwimangadzo hezwi…"* (when we see these wonders it is because of the Lord.)

Performing before the Late President of Venda

Around 1985, Bishop Masevhe was invited to perform music at the then Venda Defence Force Head Offices.

***He was privileged to play before the late Former President of Venda, Chief Minister Patrick Ramaano Mphephu, who enjoyed the performance immensely and pronounced: "I shall take him abroad."***

Later her changed his mind as he complained that the song *Muṅwe na muṅwe u ḓo fhira kha ḽino shango* – "everyone shall pass from this world" was speaking against him as the President and the other traditional leaders of that day. They complained about the part of the song which says *"na vhahulwane vha ḓo fhira "* (even the dignitaries will pass on from this world"

# PERSECUTION

***This allegation was so profound that the late Former President of Venda, Chief Minister Patrick Ramaano Mphephu, sent members of the then Special Branch of the police to come and arrest Bishop Masevhe.***

When the Special Branch members confronted him, Bishop Masevhe explained that the song was not referring to one specific person but referred to people in general including (*dziṋambi* (talented singers). Nevertheless, he stayed in jail for five days as they did not have any real case against him. They had to let him be and could not detain him any longer him.

# BEST SOLOIST ON DISK

In the year 1985 Bishop Masevhe won the Best Soloist on disk with Radio Venda with the song called *Muṅwe na muṅwe u ḓo fhira kha ḽino shango* – "everyone shall pass from this world", after beating all the artists in the former homeland of Venda.  By then, radio listeners would vote for their favourite artist by sending a greeting card to the radio station. Bishop Masevhe was informed by the radio announcers, Mr Isaac Ḓagaḓa (now a bishop) and "Razzmataz" Mr Munyai Mashige that they did not finish counting his cards, they stopped counting after the first bag became full. It was apparent that he was the most loved artist by far. He received the award at Vleifontein Hall.

*Bishop Masevhe would like to acknowledge these announcers who really promoted his music: Mr Mpho "Liṋoni" (the bird) Ṋefale, Mr Isaac Ḓagaḓa (now a bishop) and "Razzmataz" Mr Munyai Mashige.*

In 1985 he also won the Best top Gospel artist in the Northern and Eastern Transvaal with the song titled *"Dakalo"* meaning "Joy" from his gospel smash hit *"Fhungo ḽa vhuṱali na vhutshilo"* which means "the word of wisdom and life". The competition was hosted at Nkowankowa Hall in the Tzaneen area.

Both these two albums [*Muṅwe na muṅwe u ḓo fhira kha ḽino shango* – "everyone shall pass from this world" and *"Fhungo ḽa vhuṱali na vhutshilo"* meaning "the word of wisdom and life"] sold more than four hundred (400 000) copies.

The two albums were also translated into Sesotho and Isizulu languages.

In 1986, Bishop Masevhe released the album *Lufuno* (love).

# FLYING TO DURBAN

During the years 1984 - 1986, Bishop Masevhe had an Indian Pastor friend, by the name of Pastor Mohen. They were doing farm ministry in the farms in Levubu hosting a lot of Gospel Crusades. Bishop Masevhe would sing, and Pastor Mohen would preach.

Both of them were working, and in the mornings, Pastor Mohen would drive Bishop Masevhe to work at Ṱhohoyanḓou and then go to his workplace where he worked part-time for the then VDC (Venda Development Corporation).

*Later Pastor Mohen arranged for Bishop Masevhe to minister through music in Durban where Pastor Mohen was to preach at a Pentecostal Holiness Church.*

Bishop Masevhe had remained behind as he had to go to work. He boarded a public taxi to the airport in Johannesburg and flew from there to Durban.

Pastor Mohen paid for Bishop Masevhe's flight to Durban.

Bishop Masevhe flew to Durban for the first time. This was his first aeroplane ride.

*As a young boy, Bishop Masevhe never envisaged that a day would come when he would fly in an aeroplane.*

Pastor Mohen had left earlier for Durban and had taken Bishop Masevhe's keyboard to avoid Bishop Masevhe travelling by public taxi with a keyboard.

The congregation in Durban was mainly of coloured descent and did not understand the Venda songs that Bishop Masevhe sang. Before singing each song, he would explain to them what the lyrics meant.

Pastor Mohen arranged another trip to Cape Town in another Pentecostal Church.

Bishop Masevhe has fond memories of his trip to Zambia to minister at a Full Gospel Church on invitation by Bishop Muno Pedu.  Bishop Muno Pedu had seen Bishop Masevhe perform at an international conference hosted by Iron Sharpens Iron in Zambia in the presence of more than 4000 pastors.

Sometime after Zambia, Bishop Masevhe was invited to Botswana to minister at an Assemblies of God Church in Francistown.

# PLAYING REGGAE MUSIC

In 1988 Bishop Masevhe joined Decibel Music. It was one of the big recording companies being used by many famous artists who were playing traditional and reggae music then. The company signed Bishop Masevhe on the condition that he played reggae music as they did not like the music he had been playing all along.

He released a reggae album in 1988, "You are to blame", which did not perform well. The fans were confused over the sudden change in his music, not to mention the message in the album.

Maybe one may make mention here that it may have been God's way of saying to Bishop Masevhe, "this is not the kind of music I called you for so I God will sabotage you!"

In 1986 to 1987 Bishop Masevhe was transferred from the Department of Post and Telecommunications to the Department of Economic Affairs, Receiver of Revenue Section in the homeland of Venda.

In 1987 Bishop Masevhe composed and released an album in 1989 "I am free" but it was sung by Mrs Hilda Ratombo and recorded by Mdu Masilela.

# AWARDS, ACCOLADES & ALBUMS

## SECOND NATIONAL SONG FESTIVAL

It was in 1987 that Bishop Masevhe won one of his most significant awards at the second National Song Festival of South Africa.

***Bishop Masevhe came number one in the regional competition, representing the then Radio Venda and Venda with the song, "Lutendo, pfano, lufuno" (faith, unity, love). The song was a hit.***

He then represented Radio Venda and Venda in the finals in Johannesburg where he took position five (5) in the nationals. He remembers that he had performed better than some of the then famous artists like Johnny Mokgadi and Yvonne Chaka Chaka. Ricardo won the competition. He performed live on stage at the Johannesburg Standard Bank Arena.

## THIRD NATIONAL SONG FESTIVAL

Again in 1988, Bishop Masevhe won the best award under the Third National Song Festival of South Africa, in the regionals, representing the then Radio Venda with the song "In the name of love". The song performed well in the regionals.

In the nationals, the competition hosts changed the format of the competition and wanted another artist to play, the song, and that artist did not perform well, and the song did not do well.

It was the same year, 1988, when he worked for Old Mutual Insurance Company in the sales-marketing department.

## THE ALBUMS

In 1989 he recorded an album titled "*Nzumbululo* verse 20" (revelation verse 20).

In 1990 he recorded another album, "*Mudzimu a si nwana*" (God is not a child) under BK Productions, owned by Banzi Kubheka.

*He then released Greatest Hits Volume 1 and Greatest Hits Volume 2 in the same year under ROFMA Music Production (Roxley Fhatuwani Masevhe Music Production).*

In 1991 Bishop Masevhe recorded another album, "*Funa wa hau*" (Love your neighbour). One of the famous and loved songs in this album is "*Vhaporofita vha u zwifha*." False prophets).

In 1992 he released the hit "*Tshifhinga*" (Time) under Hit City Records.

Another album he released in 1992 is *Dilo tša lefase le* (the things of this world) under Hit City Records. Again in the same year, he recorded "*Luyeza yusuku*" (The day is cometh) under Hit City Records.

In 1993 he recorded another album "*Bonyongo*" (chaos) with Decibel music.

*In 1994 he released "Goya" (wild cat) with Dephon Productions under Phil Hollis. In the same year, he also released "Cape to Cairo" with RPM. Cape to Cairo was a big hit.*

During the year 1994 Bishop Masevhe joined Pastor Mutula's church in Soweto as the worship leader. He spent a long time in Johannesburg and held many crusades.

1994 he composed an album for Evans Mabasa titled "No evil no cry" under ROFMA Music Productions.

This was the time when Bishop Masevhe was still fellowshipping with Bishop Mutula.

In 1995 he released another big hit: *"Mudzimu u kunda vhaloi"* (God is stronger than witches and wizards).

In 1996 he released another album *"Banga ku palula"* (straight talk) under Notefactory Music Company.

In 1997 he released *"Ramakole Randalamo"* "Lord God Almighty).

In 1998 he released another album *"Tshiḓumbumukwe"* (Whirlwind) with the hit song *"Vhuya Lufuno lwa kale)"* (Old-time love, come back".

In 1999 he released another album *"Muya wanga"* (my soul).

In 2000 he released *"Yesu ndi khosi"* (Jesus is king) under ROFMA Music Productions.

In 2001 he released another album *"Mulanga wanga na Yeso"* (My covenant with Jesus) under ROFMA Music Productions.

In 2001, Bishop Masevhe was given a Lifetime Achievement Award for being pioneer king of Gospel Music in Limpopo. The award came with a medal by Profesional Security Training Services.

In 2002 he released *"Gundo"* (Victory) under ROFMA Music Production.

***In 2002, he produced an album to honour Thovhele Maelausumbwawahothe vho Thovhele Kennedy Tshivhase.***

He worked with the late Dalton Mbedzi. Bishop Masevhe had worked with the late Dalton Mbedzi as worshippers in many crusades while travelling with Doctor Maxwell Masakona. It was the time Doctor Maxwell Masakona was still staying at Lamondo behind the mountain (*murahu ha thavha*).

Both of them would minister with Doctor Maxwell Masakona at crusades.

***Doctor Maxwell Masakona did not own a car by then, and this crusade team would walk to gospel crusades on foot carrying the musical instruments.***

The crusade instruments were the guitar bought by Forbe's son and the galaxy speaker. It's the same instrument that Bishop Masevhe used at gospel crusades with Doctor Tshifhiwa Samson (TS) Muligwe.

# COMPOSING MUSIC FOR OTHERS

Bishop Masevhe composed songs and albums for many people. He remembers some of them but not all the details:

On these albums is called *Dumbumazikule*.

He produced an album for Junior F Masevhe named Junior Mix 1.

Vho Rejoice Mukumela sang another album composed by Bishop Masevhe and Gabriel Tshisikule.

***Bishop Masevhe also composed and produced an album for Vho Maraganedzha, a wealthy soccer club owner. The club's name was Pepsi the angel and the album name "Pepsi, the winner".***

In the year 2004, Bishop Masevhe founded Vhembe District Music Forum which fought for the rights of musicians. He is the chairperson of this organisation.

In 2005, Bishop Masevhe received Dimbanyika's Meritorious Services and Prestigious Award, presented to him by Vhembe District Municipality in the Limpopo Province.

The aim of the award was to commemorate the memory of Dimbanyika, the Vhavenda king. This is one of the notable achievement in his lifetime.

In 2007 he released *"Mudzinginyo"* (shakings) under ROFMA Music Productions.

He was the winner in the SATMA (South African Traditional Music Awards) competition with the song *"vhathu vha gole"* (the people of God).

***This was a significant award as he was voted number one by the listeners of Phalaphala FM Radio. He did not go to compete in the finals in KZN (Kwazulu Natal).***

Bishop Masevhe was busy hosting an evangelism crusade and when faced with this conflict, chose the crusade over the finals.

Bishop Masevhe also recorded an album for Reris insurance Brokers in the same year 2007 under ROFMA Music Productions.

In 2008 he released *"Mudzimu ndi mulilo"* (God is a fire) under ROFMA Music Productions.

In 2014 Bishop Masevhe released an album titled *"Mufaro Cultural Dances"* featuring Zwikona[20] (Venda male traditional dance).

---

20 Tshikona (Vendaland, 2014).

The Best Thulamela Artist awarded to him in 2014 by Thulamela Local municipality.

*In 2015 Bishop Masevhe received a Lifetime Achievement Award by Vhembe District Music Forum together with Department of Arts and Culture, Limpopo Province.*

# HONORARY DOCTORATE

*On September 24, 2016, which was on his birthday, he was conferred with an Honorary Doctorate in Creative Arts in a function hosted at UNISA*[21].

The very same year he was awarded a Life Time Achievement Award by the singing diva, Maḓuvha Madima (famous artist and TV actress) in front of the international singers Tshepo Tshola, the Village Pope, Oliver Mtukuzi and Hugh Masekela.

It was during Maduvha Madima's live performance at Worship House at Shayandima Location.

Maḓuvha Madima is the daughter of Mr Thiathu Madima, who is the source of inspiration for Bishop Masevhe. Bishop Masevhe remembers how he would emulate Mr Thiathu Madima, who used to play the concertina/piano accordion (gorostina). Mr Thiathu

---

21 (University of South Africa) one of the oldest and most reputable tertiary institutions in South Africa (Wikipedia t. f., University of South Africa, 2020).

Madima is the elder brother to Itani Madima, who is also an artist.

This recognition for his efforts was a great encouragement and an honour for Bishop Masevhe.

He regards it as one of the great highlights in his life.

On 30 September 2017, Bishop Masevhe was awarded the TSHIMA (Tshivenda Music Award) Lifetime award. The award was handed over to him by Professor Doctor Alfred Nevhutanda, Thovhele Nkhaneni Ramovha, Thovhele Gole Musiiwa Mphaphuli, the executive mayor of Vhembe District Municipality and the Mayor of Thulamela Local Municipality at the University of Venda Auditorium.

In 2018 Bishop Masevhe also received an award from Jeremia Mudau Music Production, for his Skills and development of music in the community especially his efforts in producing and promoting local talent. Jeremiah Mudau is one of Bishop Masevhe's protégé.

Bishop Masevhe received an award from Londanani HBC, Drop-in-Center in 2019 in recognition for voluntary services he rendered to the organization.

In 2019 he released the album "Mesiya" under Gabriel Tshisikule.

# OTHER AWARDS

Bishop Masevhe has received so many awards in his life that he does not remember some of the dates on which he received them, amongst others:

The Best Millennium Artist Award, an award given to him by Rihone Event Management.

A Lifetime Achievement Award was given to him by the Presbyterian Church of South Africa for his efforts in advancing gospel music in the region.

A Lifetime Award presented to him by the Community of Thengwe where he was born and bred.

A Lifetime Achievement Award was given to him by the Pentecost Healing Church.

A Lifetime Achievement Award presented to him by the Zion City Church of Shayandima for being the greatest gospel singer.

Award from Professional Security Services and Training for being the Best Gospel Artist of all the times.

# IRON SHARPENS IRON

Doctor Bishop Masevhe F. Masevhe is the Director of Music of Iron Sharpens Iron International, an Organization of Pastors and churches led by Doctor Bishop M Mbadi of Maungani Village.

# OTHER FAMOUS SONGS

Bishop Masevhe Masevhe is a music producer, music arranger, songwriter, music promoter.

*He is a prolific music composer who wrote songs such as Wanga Murena (My Lord) a Zion song he polished that has also been recorded by Joyous Celebration.*

Another song he composed is *"Nga linwe ḓuvha Jeso u do vhuya"*. In Shangaan, it is *"Siku Rinwani Jesu u ta Vuya"* (One day Jesus will come back). Many recording artists have recorded this song, amongst others, Pastor Itani Madima, Lusanda, Joyous Celebration and SCOAN worshippers are singing the song.

It is in his album titled "Amen, amen, *si zo ngena*" (Amen, amen, we will enter).

# THE INSTRUMENTALIST

Bishop Masevhe can play the keyboard, the bass guitar, drums and percussions.

He has also composed jingles music for Radio Venda, Department of Health campaigns songs and giant Insurance Companies such as Reris Insurance brokers.

# ONE MIRACLE AFTER ANOTHER

In so many instances, Bishop Masevhe has seen the hand of God intervening to save him and those who were with him. Romans 8: 28 says "And we know that all things work together for good to those who love God, to those who are the called according to His purpose." NKJV.

Psalm 23:5-6 states "You prepare a table before me in the presence of my enemies; You anoint my head with oil; My cup runs over. NKJV".

One day (he doesn't recall the year) Bishop Masevhe joined other church members as they travelled to Sibasa (about 50 kilometres (kingdom) from Thengwe), in a tractor-trailer (*gariki*), for a (UAAC) United African Apostolic Church night vigil. He danced almost the whole night, and when Bishop Masevhe felt too tired, he found a comfortable spot under the tractor-trailer (gariki) and slept.

***In the morning, the group he came with travelled away without Bishop Masevhe noticing. Fortunately for Bishop Masevhe, the tractor did not drive over him as they went away.***

Bishop Masevhe heard people talking about him saying "It is him! He is the one who was dancing last night!" "It is Fhaṱuwani, the one who was dancing last night!"

They prepared breakfast for Bishop Masevhe, meaning tea and bread, and gave Bishop Masevhe two rands (R2, 00)[22] to travel back home by bus. When Bishop Masevhe arrived home, he found his parents worried about him. Bishop Masevhe is thankful to God who protected him and ensured that the tractor carriage did not drive over him. Bishop Masevhe believes God had a reason for saving him.

Bishop Masevhe recounts an incident his parents told him about the day he nearly froze to death. His father had been playing the guitar at a party in one of the farms. It was freezing.  Bishop Masevhe was also in attendance at the party, and froze, he was not crying nor moving.

*The people who were there believed that he was dead and held him above the fire to warm him.*

As his body temperature rose, he regained consciousness and came back to life.

In another occasion, Bishop Masevhe and his friends went swimming at Mulondoḓi River Dam. They left their clothes near the dam. After swimming, as Bishop Masevhe was putting on his trousers, he felt something cold touching his leg and right then a snake fell from

---

22 In 2020 The bus fare is twenty five rands.

the trouser onto the ground but fortunately for him, it did not bite him.

There were crocodiles in the dam, but they did not attack the boys.

In another occasion, Bishop Masevhe and his friends were hunting in the mountains for an animal called *mbila*[23] rock rabbit), found mostly amongst rocks. They found one on a tree next to the school they were attending. Bishop Masevhe climbed the tree, caught it and carried it along like a puppy.

**It bit one of his fingers and clutched its teeth into the finger.**

It was as if the animal was dead but with the teeth firmly clutching his finger. Bishop Masevhe prayed and then pretended to be dead also so that the animal would release his finger and the plan worked. They then killed the animal, and Bishop Masevhe claimed that he deserved half of the animal as it had bitten him. Bishop Masevhe still has a scar on the finger.

On another occasion, Bishop Masevhe and his friends chased a cobra snake (*Phakhuphakhu*), as it ran under the stones and even when it tried to hide as much as it could they kept pursuing the animal. They chased it for some time as it was crawling in and out of various hiding places.

---

23 (Wikipedia t. f., Rock hyrax, 2020) "Rock hyrax also called Cape hyrax, rock rabbit").

These were the times when, as boys, they were living dangerously, but God protected them.

In another incident, Bishop Masevhe climbed a tree to fetch birds' eggs from its nest.

***When he looked into the birds' nest, he found himself face to face with a snake coiled inside the nest.***

Fortunately for him, the snake did not spit any poison into his eyes neither did it bite him. He was able to climb down from the tree safely.

Bishop Masevhe recalls an incident where his conspirators suspected him of doing something that offended them, but he was not only innocent, he did not know anything about the conspiracy. He was at *Chavani* Village. The conspirators lured him into the storeroom of the business where he had been performing to kill him there.

When he entered the storeroom, he found himself surrounded by tough, huge men, bouncers, armed to the teeth. Bishop Masevhe suddenly felt a surge of power come upon him and he immediately pushed the one standing by the door. He shoved the person who was busy locking the padlock of the door, pushed over the crates of bottles that were in the storeroom, and the bottles came crushing on his attackers.

***He was able to get out of the storeroom and locked the door from outside. He took off his***

*white shirt and ran for his life, fearing that they may shoot him.*

It was the soldiers from the then Venda Government, who helped him to get his sound system back. He had left everything at the venue. The soldiers suspected that whoever had attacked Bishop Masevhe had been heavily armed.

Bishop Masevhe has described his life as one miracle after another miracle.

Bishop Masevhe remembers driving from Nzhelele on a rainy day. As he approached the river, it was full. The car started sliding towards the edge of the river bank and was about to slide into the water. He quickly pulled his wife out through the driver's window, and they both escaped from falling into the river with the car.

It was a miraculous escape as he continued to see the hand of God again in his life. He believes God has appointed, called and anointed him in the evangelistic and prophetic ministry as well as the worship ministry.

In 2009 Bishop Masevhe was diagnosed with chronic tonsillitis. The doctors informed him that there was a bigger chance that he would not survive the operation. His condition was severe.

Bishop Masevhe miraculously received money for a flight and visited Prophet TB Joshua, a servant of God, in 2010, who prayed for him, after which tonsillitis disappeared from his body, even to this day. Prophet TB Joshua told Bishop Masevhe that God had already healed him while in the aeroplane, on his way to Nigeria.

Along the way, Bishop Masevhe had been praying. Prophet TB Joshua also informed Bishop Masevhe that although he loves singing a lot, he had to know that God has called him as a pastor.

# THE CALL OF BEING A PASTOR

*In 2010 after he came back, he started a church, Divine Grace Fire Temple.*

The church began to fellowship at Shayandima Location in his family yard and then moved onto Mulaudzi Building.

As the church grew, the building they had rented became small, and the church had to move to larger premises. He moved the church to Itsani Village and they fellowshipped in a soccer field in a tent for a long time. They then applied for a church site next to Thivhulawi Primary School, Itsani, Tshisaulu. They were allocated a vast land. The church has built a massive building and has more than 500 members.

The church has members travelling from far to attend church services. Some travel from Louis Trichardt, about fifty to seventy kilometers (50-70 km), away, and others travel from Tshakhuma, Mpheni, Mashau, Matsila, Nkuzana, Bungeni, Njakanjaka, Magoro, Mudziafela, Masia Village, Vuwani, Tsianda, Lwamondo (behind the mountain), Thengwe, Duthuni, Phiphidi, Mukula, Tshikonelo, Tshikweta, Bunzhe, Manamani, Dzwerani and Tshino. The church leadership is comprised of four bishops and assistant pastors.

Other branches are at Phalaborwa, Accornhoek, Bushbuckridge (led by a Bishop), Rolle Crossroads, Rolle Godide, Mukhuhlu, Buyisonto, Dwaarsloop, Francistown in Botswana (led by an apostle), and Lusaka in Zambia (led by a Bishop).

*In another incident, Bishop Masevhe was hit by a car as he was on his way from church*. After X-Ray, a doctor told him that he would be paralysed from the waist downwards, and only the upper body would function. He prayed to God, relying on bible verses, amongst others, 1 Peter 2:24, Isaiah 53:5, Exodus 15: 26 and prophesied healing on himself. He went back for X-Ray, and the paralysis report had disappeared, God had intervened and erased the negative report.

*In another car accident, at Tshakhuma, Bishop Masevhe was driving a car when the car brakes failed. He hit several cows and lost control of the vehicle, which fell into the water.*

As the car was sinking, he told the people who were travelling with him, to swim to safety.

Thanks to the Lord God Almighty, everyone survived. The vehicle had to be pulled out of the water by soldiers as all other efforts had failed. The soldiers used a helicopter to salvage the car from the water.

In another car accident, Bishop Masevhe was driving a car in Gauteng, Johannesburg CBD, when he was involved in a car accident with several vehicles. The vehicle was severely damaged and had it not been for the hand of God; Bishop Masevhe should have sustained severe injuries, if not dead. He was not injured at all.

In another car accident, in Chiawelo, Soweto, Bishop Masevhe was involved in a car accident, but he did not sustain any injuries. It was the car that was severely damaged.

One time, when Bishop Masevhe and Pastor Itani Madima were travelling to the wedding of Bishop Ṱovhowani Ramabulana, they were involved in a car accident. A drunk driver hit their car, damaging his new keyboard which was in the car.

***A screw came loose from the keyboard and lodged itself between Bishop Masevhe's teeth. Miraculously, Bishop Masevhe was not injure***d.

In another incident, Bishop Masevhe was in the queue at the Johannesburg Taxi Rank, to board a taxi from Johannesburg to Venda. When it was his turn to board the taxi, the Holy Spirit whispered to him to wait for the next one, and he obeyed. When he later reached Naboomspruit, he found out that that other taxi had been involved in a terrible accident with several fatalities.

**One of the passengers told Bishop Masevhe, "you did well by not getting into this taxi."**

Bishop Masevhe remembers using a taxi from Gauteng to travel back home in the evening. When the taxi reached Polokwane, the driver indicated that he was going to use the Giyani Route to Venda. Bishop Masevhe refused to proceed with his journey in that taxi and asked to be dropped off. He heard the Holy Spirit whisper to him "don't go." He went back home using a lift. Later, one of the passengers who was not injured, phoned him to inform him that that taxi had hit cattle and that the passengers were seriously injured.

After preaching a powerful message during a church service, Bishop Masevhe decided to pay a visit to a friend, the late Bishop Rashaka, who was the owner of Holywood Filling Station and on the way was involved in another terrible car accident. Bishop Masevhe was not hurt but was enjoying a sip of cold drink as the Police were processing the accident scene.

Bishop Masevhe recounts how one day in 1980, when he was walking from Sibasa to Phiphiḓi, Themba to visit his cousin, the late minister AA Tshivhase, of the former Venda Government, driving in his Land Rover, the one without a roof, found him along the road. His passenger was old man mushavhi Ṋetshikulwe from

Mulegane, whose daughter Muhoyo Netshikulwe (younger sister to Tondani) used to sing with Bishop Masevhe.

***The late minister AA Tshivhase stopped a public taxi that was passing by and instructed all the occupants to get out so that "Fhatuwani and his guitar could get a ride to his destination".***

The group of passengers tried to grumble against this instruction, but on seeing a gun, which was clearly visible in the Land Rover, they were forced to keep quiet. The late minister AA Tshivhase told the group "Mr Netshikulwe says he knows this young man, who is not only an excellent singer but also a good guitarist, so let him go where he needs to go."

The taxi driver was forced to turn his car around and go and deliver Bishop Masevhe to his destination, amidst much protest, and then go back to pick up his passengers. Bishop Masevhe felt so special but felt sad for the passengers who had to wait.

# A NATURAL LEADER

Bishop Masevhe's leadership skills were visible right from when he was still young at primary school when he was continuously the class and school prefect.

At High School level, he led the Student Christian Movement (SCM) until he finished high school.

Bishop Masevhe has been a board member of the South African Recording Rights Association Limited for more than twenty (20) years.

***In the year 2004, Bishop Masevhe founded Vhembe District Music Forum which fought for the rights of musicians.  He is the chairperson of this organisation.***

Bishop Masevhe was the chairperson of Limpopo Arts and Culture Federation, an organisation he founded, which fights for the rights of arts and culture artists and organisations.

Bishop Masevhe is a Chief Advisor to Chief Victor Ndwamaṱo Masevhe of the Masevhe tribe ruling the land called Madzivhanani.

Bishop Masevhe is also the chairperson of Madzivhanani-Masevhe Royal Council.

Bishop Bishop Masevhe Masevhe is now a prominent preacher who is very much sought after in South African and abroad in countries like Ghana, Kenya, Zimbabwe, Lesotho, Botswana, Namibia, and Zambia.

Bishop Masevhe used to preach on Alex TV.

He is the founder Bishop of Divine Grace Fire Temple, located at Itsani Village.

Throughout this book, we have seen Bishop Masevhe playing a leadership role in many instances, like with

ROFMA Music Productions, ROFMA Evangelical Music Ministry.

# A FARMER

Bishop Masevhe has ventured into farming, he is planting vegetables, farming cattle, goats and pigs.

# PLENTY OF CHALLENGES

There were significant challenges when he started his music because of lack of resources.

*Poverty forced him to rely on self-made instruments because he could not afford to buy equipment.*

Initially, no one had faith in what he was doing because people thought that he would never succeed.

The greatest challenge in his early days was that it was taboo to play an instrument like a guitar in a church. He faced lots of arguments wherever he was performing because the churches regarded a guitar as an instrument, which represented evil. People would tell him that a guitar could not be played during a church service as it was perceived as "the rib of the devil".

In 1980 at a Zion Church night vigil at Phiphiḓi Village, an argument ensued which led to a debate that Bishop Masevhe should not be allowed to play the guitar in that church. That debate escalated and the night vigil was disrupted and cancelled.

In his songs, Bishop Masevhe speaks directly to the listener and not in parables, e.g. "Muṅwe na muṅwe u ḓo fhira kha ḽino shango" – (everyone shall pass from this world).

This offends a lot of people, especially people who are doing what the song is cautioning against. Some feel he is singing about them. Others think he is exposing their secret sins (life). The evangelist in him surfaces a lot in his music style. Bishop Masevhe refers to himself as the "singing John the Baptist". Those who love the correction (message) in his songs, love his music to bits.

Because of this direct style of singing, he is also not invited in most music festivals. Some have developed a hatred for him. It is not only people in general, but even in some of the churches, he is viewed as a pompous singer, who is insulting people.

As mentioned above, in the book, Bishop Masevhe was arrested and stayed in jail five days by the leaders who were insisting that his songs were insulting him.

During one of his performances at Makonde, another argument arose, and Bishop Masevhe was accused of offending the listeners.

***The crowd wanted to beat him but one of his fans, a police officer, took out his gun and defended him. Bishop Masevhe was forced to run for dear life.***

It was at Maungani Village during a Lutheran Church Conference when Bishop Masevhe was performing the song "*Shangoni hu pfala zwililo*" (a cry is heard in the world) as many people are dying from abuse of alcohol. The crowd was divided, the one part shouted, "sit down, you are offending us because we enjoy drinking". The others said, "Leave him alone".

Another incident occurred during a soccer match that was being played at Ngweṇani Village at Mapholi. The crowd watching soccer at that time, heard Bishop Masevhe playing his guitar, stopped watching soccer left the field, crossed over the road and assembled around him. The headman felt disrespected and ordered that the guitar be taken away from Bishop Masevhe.

***A group of hooligans with knives once descended on a crusade in Mpandoni Village, where Bishop Masevhe was performing.***

The scuffle that followed was so nasty that even the hosting pastor had to fight off the hooligans with a stick. One of the hooligans managed to enter the church to stab Bishop Masevhe with a knife. Bishop Masevhe picked up a wooden plank and hit the person on his neck and as the man fell down the blade also fell. He bled so much that Bishop Masevhe handed himself over at the police station thinking he had killed him. When the police rushed to the scene, they found that he was still alive. This particular hooligan was a wanted criminal on parole.

In 1980 his guitar was confiscated by a Chief in Ngweṇani Ha-Mapholi for performing in the village without a permit.

In 1981 his guitar was taken away by a taxi owner-driver in Lwamondo for singing inside his taxi.

*In 1982 he escaped being beaten by a mob for singing songs which they did not like in the village of Makonde, he was rescued by an off duty policeman*.

In 1980 at a Lutheran Church conference at Beuster he was yelled down by part of the crowd who did not like his songs.

While singing at Thohoyandou Stadium, the then security apparatus of the former Venda Government muted his microphone.

In 1985 while performing at Muwaweni Village, with his eyes closed, deep in the spirit, a person threw a large rock at him. By the time Bishop Masevhe opened his eyes, he was surprised seeing members of the crowd beating this person mercilessly. Upon enquiry, the group told Bishop Masevhe "the person had nearly killed the Pastor". He asked the crown, "which Pastor?" and they responded "you".

Bishop Masevhe was later informed by those who were watching that when the stone reached his face, it changed direction, hit the steel part of a window. Bishop Masevhe defended the person, telling the crown that it was a miracle for a stone to change course in mid-air, especially when it had reached its intended target.

*Although he recorded so many albums, there was a huge language barrier which made his music not to sell in the other regions of South Africa.*

Currently, the challenge of piracy is killing music sales as pirated music is filling the pavements of South Africa and the rest of the world.

Bishop Masevhe recalls how on another occasion he travelled from Johannesburg in Gauteng for a performance at the Thohoyandou Stadium.

*When he arrived, the promoter told him he had arrived late and was not allowed to sing. He had hired a combi (passenger van) to travel from Gauteng. He was not paid and had to borrow money to return to Gauteng. A sad memory for Bishop Masevhe.*

He once travelled to Nkomo Village to perform at a wedding celebration. Bishop Masevhe had bought a handsome white suit for the occasion. They arrived at the venue in the evening, and when they were busy offloading their bags from the car into the house, his suit disappeared. It was a frustrating moment in his life. Finally, the villagers were able to trace the thief and recover the suit.

Another painful memory for Bishop Masevhe is the period when Dean Farisani had been chased away from Venda (former Venda Homeland) as persona non grata. Dean Farisani was told to travel overseas. Dean Tshenuwani Farisani was receiving farewell gifts, traditional vegetables (miroho), Mopani worms, and other things he needed for his trip to America.

*Bishop Masevhe recalls how he cried so much after the goodbye farewell for Dean Farisani, held at Doctor Ramasuvha's place. He loved Dean Tshenuwani Farisani so much, and the feeling was mutual.*

There was one church conference, which was scheduled to be held at Khubvi Village but was cancelled because of the 1977/78 political violence. The late Pastor Makhari's child had passed away around that time, and he decided to use the funeral to cater to the already planned church conference. The funeral was sad as the pastor had lost his child, but it was a blessing for Christians. The powers that be then, the police and the white police officials seconded to Venda had refused permission for the church conference to be held.

# THE HIGHLIGHTS

One of the good things that Bishop Masevhe remembers is when the late Former President of Venda, Chief Minister Patrick Ramaano Mphephu, undertook to buy musical instruments for Bishop Masevhe. The Former President made this undertaking after he had seen Bishop Masevhe's performance and decided to reward him. The late Former President of Venda, Chief Minister Patrick Ramaano Mphephu invited Bishop Masevhe to come to his palace in Nzhelele.

When he arrived, the late Former President of Venda, Chief Minister Patrick Ramaano Mphephu, told Bishop Masevhe, jokingly so, that the chiefs (mahosi) wanted the police to arrest Bishop Masevhe. They accused Bishop Masevhe of singing that they (the traditional leaders (mahosi)) and everyone will die, especially those of high profile. He further told Bishop Masevhe that he, the late Former President of Venda, Chief Minister Patrick Ramaano Mphephu, had responded to inform the people that "This boy is not referring to you traditional leaders, but he is referring to everybody".

Bishop Masevhe recalls how the late Former President of Venda, Chief Minister Patrick Ramaano Mphephu, reached under his table and brought out a bundle of notes and handed them to him. Bishop Masevhe suspected it was monies that people would give to the late Former President of Venda, Chief Minister Patrick Ramaano Mphephu to show their allegiance to him (monies for nduvho). He received around two thousand rands, which was a lot of money in 1984 and it was immediately after his wedding. He and his wife were still on honeymoon.

Bishop Masevhe told the late Former President of Venda, Chief Minister Patrick Ramaano Mphephu, that even though he was making money out of performances, his wife was unemployed. The late Former President of Venda, Chief Minister Patrick Ramaano Mphephu asked Bishop Masevhe about his wife's educational background. It was during the weekend. The late former President then told Bishop Masevhe, "Your wife is hired, bring her on Monday." And that is how Bishop Masevhe's wife got employed. This favour was also extended to Bishop Masevhe's father in law, who was later employed by the then Venda government in the cattle dip (dipeni) (dip (Wikipedia, the free encyclopedia, 2019)) area.

### His music is receiving a high volume of airplay in Botswana.

He has many prominent and well-known fans, amongst others, Khosikhulu vho Tony Mphephu, Thovhele Gole Mphaphuli, Thovhele Mashamba, Thovhele A Manenzhe, Vhavenda Vho Mubalanganyi Davhula, Tshifhe David Thidiela, Doctor Mashango Mbadi, and many others.

Bishop Masevhe's boys are following in their fathers' footsteps: Fhatuwani has recorded two albums, which were produced by Bishop Masevhe. Mukano has released a single which was produced by Mushanzhi.

Fhatuwani Junior plays the bass guitar while Mukano plays the keyboard, and Mukhuthadzi plays the drums.

# DISAPPOINTMENTS

Bishop Masevhe sadly remembers his experiences with Minc Records. His album, *"Muṅwe na muṅwe u ḓo fhira* [everyone will pass from this world]" was the buzz word of that time and he knew that people were buying copies like crazy.

**To his utter surprise, he received low paycheques (two, three and seven thousand rands) from the recording company.**

He had the same experience with his album, *"Goya"* (wild cat), the album made good sales, but he received peanuts in royalties.

**Bishop Masevhe acknowledges that when he was under RPM Records, he was paid well.**

Hit City Records Company was another disaster. The company was owned by John Gananakis and Banzi Kubheka. It was so hard for Bishop Masevhe to receive any royalty payments from them.

He recalls how they would just give him a box of his CDs and tell him to go sell the CDs.

They would arrange cheap hotel accommodation (usually the type highly populated by prostitutes) for him and give him about two thousand rands for fuel to go back home. These were painful experiences.

Some artist promoters do not care about their clients. One time, RPM records took him and others to promote Albasini Dam in Musina. The artist line-up was of different genres of music. The event was held in a tavern and Bishop Masevhe, a pastor, was singing gospel music.

After the event, the promoters booked all the performers, in one hotel room and brought girls to the room. During the night, some of the artists were drinking alcohol, while others were having sex.

***This was disappointing and shameful for Bishop Masevhe.***

He remembers how during the night, he was awakened, by a hand caressing him, only to wake up to find a girl trying to seduce him into having sex with her. He told the girl that he is a pastor, and that is why he was sleeping in his suit.

He also remembers one music festival where he had performed with Colbert Mukwevho, Paul Ndlovu, Condry Siqubu, and Step Ahead. The venue was full, but after the event, the promoter was nowhere to be found. The artists had to trace the promoter's whereabouts, and even then, it was a struggle to receive what was due to them.

***Each artist was paid two hundred and fifty rands (R250) for the performance.***

Bishop Masevhe has rubbed shoulders and shared stage with the cream of the crop in South African music, superstars such as Yvonne Chaka Chaka with whom he shared the stage at Ṱhohoyanḓou stadium in front of a crowd of forty-five (45 000) people.

He has shared the stage with the late Paul Ndlovu, the late Albert Mundalamo Tshikundamalema, South African Super Stars, Dan Tshanḓa, Chicco Twala, Colbert Mukwevho, Arthur Mafokate, Pastor Itani Madima, the late Brenda Fassie, CJB, Blondie and Pappa Makhene, Doctor Thomas Chauke, Penny-Penny, Sipho Makhabane, Rebecca Malope, the late Mzwakhe Mbuli, Stimela, Ray Phiri, Mdu, Sipho Hotstix Mabuse, Solly Moholo, the late Mpho Regalo, Echo and many more.

***He has regularly performed during Mapungubwe Arts and Cultural Festivals with other famous artists like Zola (at Peter Mokaba Stadium in Polokwane). This is an annual festival hosted by the Limpopo Provincial Government.***

Bishop Masevhe recalls how on another occasion he travelled from Johannesburg in Gauteng for a performance at the Thohoyandou Stadium.

# SOWING BACK INTO THE COMMUNITY

Bishop Masevhe knows how tough and rough it is growing without funds for tuition fees. He appreciates the fact that his parents were not able to send him to school and how Doctor VS Ramasuvha and Mr Andries Makhitha Neswiswa helped him by paying his school fees.

***It is for this reason that he also makes sure that he helps students in need.***

One such young man is Mashudu Matika, who wanted to be an artist, who viewed Bishop Masevhe as his role model. Bishop Masevhe helped him to study music in Johannesburg.  Mashudu Matika is now a pastor and also a singer.

Gabriel Tshisikule approached Bishop Masevhe to tell him that he wanted to study music. He travelled around with Bishop Masevhe performing, ministering singing. Bishop Masevhe started helping Gabriel with pocket money, books and other necessities as a student.

Bishop Masevhe paid for his tuition fee to study music. Mr Gabriel Tshisikule is now a highly respected music producer with a big recording studio in Gauteng, a music engineer of note. He has engineered sound for members of Soul Brothers and the late Lucky

Dube. Gabriel Tshisikule promotes local music and local artists overseas.

After Bishop Masevhe started his ministry, Divine Grace Temple Church in Itsani, he assembled about fifteen (15) local boys who had repented at church and started mentoring them and accommodated them at the church. Some were drug addicts others drunkards and other no-good boys. He would buy food for them. The boys started to change and are now much older, and almost all of them are working. Amongst them are builders and bricklayers.

Bishop Masevhe helped another young lady by paying for her tuition fee to study to become a security guard and another to become a nurse.

Currently (2020), there is one young man, Omphulusa Ragimana, who is in Grade 12 and Bishop Masevhe is taking care of him.

***Some of the people Bishop Masevhe helped are managers. He ensures that he encourages young people to study and make something of their lives.***

Bishop Masevhe has unearthed artists such as the late Emmanuel Mamphogoro who was a highly respected music producer, sound engineer for various top stars and live DVD recordings in South Africa.

***Rofhiwa Manyaga is one of the artists that were mentored by Bishop Masevhe.***

He travelled with Bishop Masevhe on many crusades. He would either be a backing vocal or playing instruments. Rofhiwa has admitted that he has learned a lot from Bishop Masevhe.

Bishop Masevhe also mentored Tshifhiwa Tancred Ṋetshiongolwe with whom he also travelled when they were ministering.

Mrs Daphney Masevhe was part of the backing vocals in the following albums: Tshiḓumbumukwe (Whirlwind), Ramakole Randalamo (Lord God Almighty), and Gundo (Victory).

***Bishop Masevhe has unearthed and developed top international gospel artist, Rejoice Thina Mukumela whose first gospel album was composed and produced by Bishop Masevhe.***

Bishop Masevhe has unearthed and developed young diva called Fhulu Ḓangale who has recently toured America with Worship House.

Bishop Masevhe has helped many recording artists nationally and regionally. Some own recording companies such as Dan Ṋetshakhuma, Patrick Matsila, who owns a music marketing and distributing company, Eric Ḽiphadzi, who is also involved in the Film and Video making industry.

Hilda Ratombo is the first female gospel artist to play a keyboard and record music,

She acknowledges that Bishop Masevhe trained her to play the keyboard. There were 3 girls: Hilda Ratombo, Doris Thabo and Patricia Muthavini who loved Bishop Masevhe's music. These girls participated much in the ROFMA gospel crusades and conferences and learnt a lot along the way. It helped these girls to grow in faith, and they met a lot of pastors. The other two ladies dropped out of the group, but Hilda Ratombo remained behind. She acknowledges that Bishop Masevhe helped her to get a job at the Public Service Commission. He is the one who submitted her CV for the job application, and she was eventually hired.

She has observed that most of the things he said or prophesied in his songs have come to pass.

Hilda Ratombo has recalled that Bishop Masevhe is the first person to invite Benjamin Dube to come to Venda. By then Benjamin Dube was still young, and they were performing as Dube Family. The festival was held at Makwarela Hall. The Dube family came in a Hi-Ace and slept over in Maungani at Beuster.

***She further recalls that Bishop Masevhe is also the first person to invite Doctor Elija Maswanganyi to Venda.  This was around 1985.***

Bishop Masevhe has also helped Junior M and many more.

From the 90's up to now he was a board member of South African Recording Rights Association Limited (SARRAL) He has retired from this organisation.

Bishop Masevhe's spiritual womb was carrying a lot of talent, anointing and people, and one begins to have an idea as to why God would save his life so many times.

# MENTORS

Bishop Masevhe has been mentored by many great men and women of God. Due to the nature of his ministry, Bishop Masevhe socialised with lots of people of a different calibre.

*Doctor Jonas Ntshavheni Bvumbi of Maṉiini Baptist Church taught Bishop Masevhe the word of God and how to live an exemplary life.*

Bishop Masevhe remembers how he experienced crippling challenges in his life and was at the lowest point of his life, which led to the breakdown of his marriage and divorce. This was a painful moment of his life.

*It was Doctor Jonas Ntshavheni Bvumbi and his wife, Doctor Jonas Ntshavheni Bvumbi, who brought him back to life. They never forsook him. Bishop Masevhe was down and out and had lost hope. The couple made sure to follow up on him and worked hard to guide Bishop Masevhe back to life and life with Christ.*

He referred to the couple, as a couple full of love. For Bishop Masevhe, their act of love was like they picked him up from the muddy road, cleaned him up and put him back on track with life again.

*Another pastor who helped him become stronger when things had really gone from bad to worse is old lady, Pastor Jombere of Tswinga of whom Bishop Masevhe spoke fondly and referred to her as a mother.*

Bishop Masevhe knows that more often than not, most servants of God are not good at helping fallen brethren, Instead of helping, most of them will finish you up.

Bishop Muṱula, of Calvary Church in Soweto, is another Pastor who helped Bishop Masevhe when he was down and out. When Bishop Masevhe had nothing, Bishop Muṱula rented a big house for Bishop Masevhe, bought food for him and helped him to get back on track. In return, Bishop Masevhe helped Bishop Muṱula by raising funds for the church to build an auditorium.

*Another person who helped to nail the final nail to Bishop Masevhe's divorce woes was Apostle Maxwell Masakona.*

Bishop Masevhe describes him as the prophet of his life. He is the one who gave him the prophecy in 2009, for crossover into 2010.

*By then, Bishop Masevhe had nothing, no car no money and had even travelled to the prayer session by lift.*

The moment Bishop Masevhe entered the church, Apostle Maxwell Masakona spoke prophetically into his life. He said "Watch Roxley in 2010, watch him" and the moment the year 2009 started his life immediately turned around.

He bought cars, BMW 525, BMW 525. BMW 740, BMW 520i and Mercedes Benz 320. This was after he had been struggling since the year 1989. This was such a relief because, during that period, most of the pastors had pushed him away and would despise him and be sarcastic against him.

*The situation was painful. There were times when Bishop Masevhe would be invited to perform at certain events, and some of the pastors would speak against him and try to influence the host to remove him from the program.*

Some of the pastors would speak against him and try to influence the host to remove him from the program.

***In Bishop Masevhe's words "May God bless this pastor and add many more years to his life."***

The father of Doctor Jonas Ntshavheni Bvumb, priest (Tshifhe) Livhebe, of Maṋiini Baptist Church is one of the old men who shaped Bishop Masevhe's life. He taught him how to live for Jesus Christ and how to be born again.

Pastor Regina Makhuvha of Mapate Assemblies of God is one of the old ladies that contributed to Bishop Masevhe's spiritual growth.

***Pastor Athalia Mavhutha (now Doctor Athalia Mavhutha) was instrumental in that she was a mother to Bishop Masevhe and instructed him in the way of life.***

The late Doctor Maswole Ragimana of Faith Mission Church is the one under whose authority Bishop Masevhe was baptised in the year 1978 by Pastor Sadiki.

Bishop Masevhe ministered many a time with Pastor Mushapho (now Doctor Mushapho) of the Will of God Church, at Siloam Village and planted a lot of churches at Lambani. Bishop Masevhe would be ministering through music during the crusades.

***Pastor Siphuma of Makwarela Full Gospel Church made a lot of positive input in Bishop Masevhe's life.***

Pastor Maḽori Mavhetha of Folovhoḓwe Nazarene helped Bishop Masevhe to live the life of loving Jesus Christ.

Professor Alfred Ṋevhutanda of Tshivhiliḓulu Faith Mission and Dopeni Faith Mission Churches, by then, even bought a keyboard for Bishop Masevhe. He is one father who guided Bishop Masevhe to live a life of Christ.

Dean Tshenuwani Farisani and the late Reverend Phosiwa of Maungani also guided Bishop Masevhe and also introduced him to politics.

*Dean Tshenuwani Farisani was also responsible for facilitating the purchase of a galaxy guitar speaker for Bishop Masevhe. The speaker was donated by Evangelical Church Donors from Germany (The son of Forbe).*

Doctor Tshifhiwa Samson (TS) Muligwe, with whom he ministered many times in Crusades and conferences. Was a great source of inspiration, together with his wife, Pastor Paulina Muligwe.

*Bishop Masevhe admitted that most of the lyrics for most of his songs were influenced by the messages of Doctor Tshifhiwa Samson (TS) Muligwe.*

When Doctor Tshifhiwa Samson (TS) Muligwe would be busy preaching, Bishop Masevhe would be composing songs. Bishop Masevhe is ever thankful to Doctor Tshifhiwa Samson (TS) Muligwe for bailing him out of Maṱatshe Prison. This was after he was arrested for failing to replace a generator that was accidentally burned during a crusade by one of the crusade crew member, Mashudu Matika (now a pastor) who was a youth by then.

The owner of the generator wanted it to be replaced. At that time, there was no electricity and people relied on generators. Various pastors who had organised that particular crusade in Nzhelele Tshavhalovhedzi in 1985, agreed that fundraising was to be made for the purchase of the generator. Some of the pastors who had agreed to help did not honour their commitments, and Bishop Masevhe was the only one paying. *Along the way, he could no longer afford to continue and was then arrested and imprisoned at Maṱatshe Prison for two weeks until Doctor TS Muligwe came to his rescue.*

Bishop Masevhe's prayer life was shaped by the late Reverend Pastor Mahamba of Khubvi and Pastor Lawrence Takalani of Sokotenda. They would wake them up in the early hours of the morning to pray. They taught him and his friends that education is essential. They advised the young men to start small scale farming to help finance the work of God.

The old man, the late Pastor Makhari of Ngweṋani helped to shape Bishop Masevhe's life.

Pastor Lennox Ṋemukula played a crucial role in Bishop Masevhe's life.

*His brother, Pastor Lawrence Ṋemukula, was used by God to reveal to Bishop Masevhe that Jesus Christ is alive. These servants of God are Pastor Athalia Mavhutha's brothers.*

Doctor Boy Mbedzi, played a role in shaping Bishop Masevhe's gift of ministering through music.

Bishop Masevhe is grateful for the role played by Bishop Doctor Sam Ndadza, with whom he travelled a lot and for his mentorship role in his life.

He also acknowledges Bishop Madanda his friend. They attended school together.

Reverend Silas Ṋefefe taught Bishop Masevhe the word of God.

Professor Doctor Rabali was instrumental in teaching Bishop Masevhe about hospital evangelism ministry.

Bishop Mulaudzi of Mulaudzi Bus Service was a church leader, and Bishop Masevhe learnt a lot from him.

Some of the International men of God who worked with Bishop Masevhe are Pastor Mohen from Australia, Apostle Naison Kamusha, Bishop Booker Munopedu from Zambia, Apostle Dr Vincent Victous from the

USA, Bishop Kamona of Zambia, Bishop Kamusha Botswana.

These men and women of God have made positive inputs into the life of Bishop Masevhe during different times. They have collectively helped to shape him to become the man, husband, singer, worshipper, pastor and artist that he is today. He is full of gratitude to God for using them to shape his life. These are people that Bishop Masevhe will never forget in his lifetime.

# FRIENDS

*Bishop Masevhe has had many friends throughout his life.*

In primary school, his best friend was Moses Marubini. Both were excellent students and would compete for position one at school.

Another friend, Marcus Munyai, like Bishop Masevhe, loved reading books.

Bishop Masevhe met most of his friends in his walk in the Lord.

The late Joas Murabi, a friend of Bishop Masevhe who also loved singing, was an excellent singer.

Another friend he met in the work of God is, the late Ntsedzeni Rambuda.

Pax Muhali, then a teacher, was Bishop Masevhe's close friends is now Pastor at Faith Mission Church.

Isaac Ndou from Musina, welcomed Bishop Masevhe in Musina when Bishop Masevhe was selling CDS and desperate for accommodation. Bishop Masevhe had travelled to Musina in a taxi. He accommodated me and transported me in his car. Bishop Masevhe had been disappointed by the person who had agreed to accommodate him.

Boxing Sebola welcomed Bishop Masevhe in Tzaneen as he was busy marketing his music.

Reverend Maphophe, of the Assemblies of God church, is a close friend, of Bishop Masevhe.

The late Bishop Joseph Makwakwa was another close friend of Bishop Masevhe.

The late Muvhuso Mudzanani, who met Bishop Masevhe on business, was also a close friend.

Bishop Masevhe's neighbour, the late Mukwevho, was another close friend.

The late Portio Mokoni, was younger than Bishop Masevhe but was his close friend.

The late Khwaṱhisani Ratshiṱanga, an artist, is another young close friend of Bishop Masevhe and loved Mzwakhe Mbuli's music.

The Archbishop Elect, Bishop Mbangiseni Ratshiṱanga was a close friend of Bishop Masevhe and an elder brother of Khwaṱhisani Ratshiṱanga. Initially, Bishop Masevhe was friends with the brother,. When Archbishop Elect, Bishop Mbangiseni Ratshiṱanga started working as a nurse, Bishop Masevhe drew closer to the brother, Chief Lutshekule Rathiṱanga, now a Chief, of Ngulumbi, Phiphidi. Chief Lutshekule Rathiṱanga used his car to transport Bishop Masevhe to many places.

Another close friend is Kennedy Sitsula, now an advocate. The friend who gave him his first guitar.

Other close friends of Bishop Masevhe are Nthumeni Ligamela, Siṱhari and Eric Ailwei Shavhani.

The late Avhatakali Justice Dzhalagome, from Ngweṋani, helped Bishop Masevhe get his guitar back after it was confiscated during the soccer match at Ngweṋani.

Thiathu Ṱuwani, from Thengwe, and a politician, is another young friend of Bishop Masevhe.

The late Bishop Rashaka, a businessman, who owned Hollywood Motors Garage, was another close friend of Bishop Masevhe.

The late Alfred Ṋetshidzivhani had worked with Bishop Masevhe to recruit clients for insurance policies.

Another excellent singer, Bishop Frank Ndadza, stays at Tshino travelled with Bishop Masevhe for music ministry.

Joe Maombe, a businessman, (cash loans business) is a close friend of Bishop Masevhe.

Nkhanedzeni Manenzhe is a fan and a close friend of Bishop Masevhe.

Mathavha, a businessman, is another close friend of Bishop Masevhe and owns and leases residential houses.

Vuledzani Joseph Mukhwathi from Mpandoni is a younger brother and close friend of Bishop Masevhe.

Bishop Masevhe taught Collins Sethlavane, about music and they are still friends.

The late Sam Ṋemaḓoḓani, a police officer, was a close friend of Bishop Masevhe.

The late Fhaṱuwani Manyage was inspired to play music by Bishop Masevhe and became a close friend of Bishop Masevhe. He was a taxi driver.

Fhaṱuwani Ṋetshamulivho was Bishop Masevhe's relative and close friend. They used to carve toy cars from Mulevhu tree.

Pastor Thivhavhoni Ḽidzhade (now a Pastor) is another close friend.

Michael Ṱhavhana (now a Pastor) is a close friend with whom he shared lots of personal issues. Bishop Masevhe remembers that Michael Ṱhavhana was a strict friend and that if one visited him without alerting him, one would possibly find oneself sleeping outside. Bishop Masevhe recalls that he was the exception to this rule and he would be allowed inside the High Point Building flat in Hillbrow without prior appointment.

Jane Mashamba, sister to Chief Mashamba, was a teacher, is a close friend of Bishop Masevhe. She is now Mrs Munyai.

Ndivhuho Mugivhi, a teacher, now married, is a close friend of Bishop Masevhe.

Mushavhi Edward Phaṱhela was a close friend.

Godfrey Ṋenzhelele, now a Baptist church minister is a close friend of Bishop Masevhe. Bishop Masevhe recalls eating mangoes and having drinks with him at Folovhoḓwe.

Christopher Demana, a close friend of Bishop Masevhe, also attended Thengwe High School with Bishop Masevhe.

George Gemeli, a teacher, who plays the guitar and stays in Nzhelele is a close friend of Bishop Masevhe.

Tshifhiwa from Nzhelele is a close friend of Bishop Masevhe.

Aluwani Muyanalo is a close friend of Bishop Masevhe.

Simon Munyai, a designer and dressmaker, is a close friend of Bishop Masevhe. Bishop Masevhe recalls how they would open a can of fish with lukwea (a tool used for cutting grass) because they did not have a knife.

Pastor Simon Mpfariseni Munyai, an artist, is a close friend of Bishop Masevhe. Bishop Masevhe remembers that this friend used to give him beautiful shirts.

Fhaṱuwani Mushavhi Ṋemathaga from Lufule, a photographer, loves Bishop Masevhe so much and is a close friend of Bishop Masevhe.

The late Ailwei from Tshisaulu used to play music with Bishop Masevhe and was a close friend of Bishop Masevhe.

Fhulu Makhuvha attended Thengwe High School with Bishop Masevhe and is still a close friend of Bishop Masevhe. She is the daughter of Pastor Reginah Makhuvha and introduced Bishop Masevhe to her mom, who supported the ministry of Bishop Masevhe significantly.

Shumani Ṋefale from Duthuni was a close friend of Bishop Masevhe and buys all the CDs of Bishop Masevhe.

The late Dziedzi Maphiri was a close friend of Bishop Masevhe,

Pastor Ngobeni from Malamulele is a close friend of Bishop Masevhe.

An old-time friend with whom Bishop Masevhe attended the Pentecostal Holiness conferences, Tshifhe Sam Mametsa under Pastor Maswanganyi and Pastor Mpikanyisi and the late Reverend Magayisa.

The late Dalton Mbedzi, a music composer and excellent artist, was a close friend of Bishop Masevhe.

Pastor John Ramulumbi, who travelled in ministry with Bishop Masevhe is a close friend of Bishop Masevhe.

Mr Ramunyisi, who is a zionist, is still a fan and close friend of Bishop Masevhe.

Through it, all, Bishop Masevhe has learned that you never forsake your friends because you are doing well in life.

# TESTIMONIES

The music ministry of Bishop Masevhe has touched and transformed many lives. There is plenty of testimonies to this effect and below are just a few of them:

# MRS REJOICE THINA MUKUMELA

"The first time I saw Bishop Masevhe performing was at a youth camp. I was not born again, but I loved singing.

*My love for music and the way he performed his music ministry and played the guitar forced me to hang around as I wanted to know more about this man and his music.*

He composed my first album, and he and Mrs Daphney Masevhe were part of my backing vocals for that album.

I thank him for his encouragement that has bought growth in my music ministry. I say to Doctor R F Masevhe, let the show go on.

# GABRIEL "THE GREAT" TSHISIKULE

"I have a studio, GTB Productions. I know Bishop Masevhe for a long time now. I have worked so much with this servant of God.

Around 1990, I think, I was in Standard 8 a friend of mine, the late Bethuel Khathutshelo Mukwevho "mufambisa ntiro" ( Mr MC/programme director ) introduced me to Bishop Masevhe.

I remember that every Friday of my secondary school years, I would rush from home, at Miluwani, after school, to Ṱhohoyanḓou, Bears Furniture Shop. I knew I would find Bishop Masevhe promoting the Furniture Shop. Afterwards, I would help him to carry the instruments.

*I stayed with him, and this helped me so much in my career. I learned much about music. I passed matric in 1992.*

In 1993 I was working with Bishop Masevhe full time, he taught me how to record. He was recording with a Technics radio, CD320 (with excellent quality) and he also had technics keyboard. We recorded a lot of people. Some recorded full albums, and for others, it was just a single. We recorded Tancred Netshiongolwe's first album and Emmanuel Mamphogoro's first album.

I remember we were later joined by the late Jeffery Mulaudzi who came with his Yamaha V50 Keyboard.

I was the first to learn how to programme this keyboard. We recorded beautiful music with this keyboard.  I met a lot of famous artists during this period.

*In 1994 Bishop Masevhe helped me to register with the Univesity of Venda, to study music. This is how I rose up in my career.*

In 1995 I went to Durban Westville to further my studies.

The first time I entered a proper recording studio in Johannesburg was when Bishop Masevhe was recording an album with Banzi Kubheka. I was one of the instrumentalists for that album. It gave me a beautiful opportunity to learn the studio recording process. Julius Mudau, the engineer, who was so friendly and patient with my million questions, taught me a lot about the studio equipment. I was so excited.

We went back again to Johannesburg to record the album for Mrs Rejoice Mukumela. Bishop Masevhe gave me the role to producer the album, and I subsequently produced three of her albums.

I set up my own studio GTB Productions in Yeoville, Johannesburg around 1997 /98 and have since then recorded a lot of people. I have recorded some of Bishop Masevhe's albums, e.g. *Vhuya Lufuno lwa kale* (Old-time love come back).

**Bishop Masevhe is a great encourager, and if you are willing, he allows you to showcase your skills.**

Bishop Masevhe has referred a lot of artists to me for recording.

I have been to the USA, Europe, and France. Whilst travelling in the USA I found a JVC Keyboard, the same keyboard model that Bishop Masevhe had. I had never seen it before, but Bishop Masevhe would tell us beautiful stories about that keyboard. I ordered it for him, and when I surprised him with the gift, he was overjoyed. Both of us were crying. The old JVC keyboard was famous. I recall hearing listeners on Phalaphala FM referring to Bishop Masevhe as Roxley Masevhe and his golden keyboard.

**Had it not been for Bishop Masevhe, where would I be, I wonder?"**

# EVANGELIST TSHIMANGADZO MAEMU

"I started following Bishop Masevhe and listening to his music in 1994. I listened to the album *Tshifhinga* (time).

**In February of 1982, I was touched and transformed by the song A huna Mulalo kha vha sa tendiho Mudzimu (There is no peace for those who do not believe in God). From then on, I started to attend church at Kutama Pentecostal Holiness Church. On 30 May 1999, I was baptised by Pastor Lorraine Luvhengo.**

I am thankful for his effort in my life, maybe I would be dead, but now I stand in front of people and preach Jesus Christ with confidence. May God bless Bishop Masevhe. I remember an outstanding performance by Bishop Masevhe at the Mapungubwe Arts Festival in 2008 at Polokwane.

**Most of the artists who performed before him**

*were miming and playing background music, but when Doctor R F Masevhe ascended the stage he was singing live, and this revived the crowd. I really enjoyed that performance."*

## SLENDER GIRL, AN UP AND COMING ARTIST

"I love and enjoy the music of Doctor R F Masevhe. When I am sad, I listen to the song *Lufuno* (Love), and it always lifts my spirit. His music is full of life and energy. To Doctor R F Masevhe, your music brings joy and happiness to my life. I am your greatest fan."

## MISS AVHEANI NYATHELA

"I met Doctor R F Masevhe when he prayed for my mom, who was sick and on the point of dying. She was healed, and that is how I came to love him and his music. When I met him, I had been looking for a job for years. He said to me, I do not care that you have been told you will never be employed, you will find employment. I can testify that I a now employed and thankful to God for using Doctor R F Masevhe to transform my life."

## ELDER MUBALANGANYI DAVHULA

"I ask that you place the white guitar that Pastor Sitsula gave to you in your music museum. Yours is not only an anointing, but it is also your heritage, the heritage of the Vhavenda people and the other nations of the whole world. I say *"Tsha u fa kule"*, and I wish that you would compose another song called "Khube" (face mask). The year 2020 has left terrible consequences. What do we behold in this year? I thank you, Bishop Masevhe."

## REVIVED FROM A COMA

The elder brother to Professor Doyoyo, was in a coma, and someone played him one of Bishop Masevhe's songs, *Mbilalelo dzaṋu* (Your worries). On hearing the music, the man was revived out of coma and was healed.

# AGAINST ALL ODDS

Bishop Masevhe was on fire from the womb. The poverty tried to stop him from manifesting his gifts, but he denied poverty that joy. He took a can of oil/ paraffin and wood and made a guitar for himself.

People did not see any potential future in him, but that did not stop or discourage Bishop Masevhe from forging ahead in full force.

***When his shoes were too old or torn, he took a wire and sew them back together.***

When he did not have money to travel anywhere, he used what God gave him, instead of four wheels (a car) he used his two wheels (feet) and walked to where he needed to go.

*When there was no food in the house, he used his two hands either to plant food or to work for someone else to bring home an income. If all failed, he would go the veld and catch a meal for the day.*

These traits are hard to find nowadays.

It was rough growing up, and he needed other people to move on in life. Now that he has moved on, he has not forgotten his past. He helps others to move on in life.

Bishop Masevhe has refused to die so many times it can only be by the grace of God Almighty in heaven that he is still going strong 61 years later.

*The man refused to go hungry when nature is full of healthy delicacies like grasshoppers, fruits and wild animals which God in his omniscient omnipotent and omnipresent power[24] has provided.*

He has been cheated and lied to, used and jailed, but he refused to remain down on the floor.

---

24 Omnipotence means God is all-powerful. This means God has supreme power and has no limitations. Omniscience means God is all-knowing. Omnipresence means God is everywhere at the same time. (Study.com, 2003-2020).

He sacrificed himself to send his siblings to school and give them a better chance at life: the one brother is now a manager in a government department.

When there was no paraffin, no candles and no electricity, he went outside and used the moonlight to study or sat by the fire and used the light from the fire as his study lamp.

*Sixty-one (61) years later and Bishop Masevhe is now a multi-award winning artist.*

# PLEASE NOTE

Bishop Masevhe acknowledges that he has been in contact with many people throughout his life and ministry and may not have added some people and events as yet. He will continue to compile more information as he remembers so that it can be added to the book to give a complete picture.

**ROFMA STATIONERY**

# ALBUMS & SONGS

## LIST OF CRUSADES 1985

THE ROFMA EVANGELICAL MUSIC MINISTRIES

Box 774

SIBASA

VENDA

| PROGRAM | 1985 | |
|---|---|---|
| 1. 2 — 13 Jan. | CRUSADE | PHADZIMA |
| 2. 8 — 10 Feb. | CRUSADE REVIVAL | GIYANI (Noblehoek) |
| 3. 1 — 3 March | CRUSADE REVIVAL | GAZANKULU |
| 4. 24 — 26 MAY | REVIVAL CRUSADE | MATSHENA |
| 5. 21 — 23 JUNE | Marriage. love and courtship conf. | Tshipise |
| 6. 17 — 23 JuNE | CRUSADE | TSHAMHALOVHEDZI |

As at July 2020, Bishop Masevhe has released around forty five (45) albums and has recorded/composed more than seven (700) songs. Some of which are no

**PERMISSION TO USE FACILITIES**

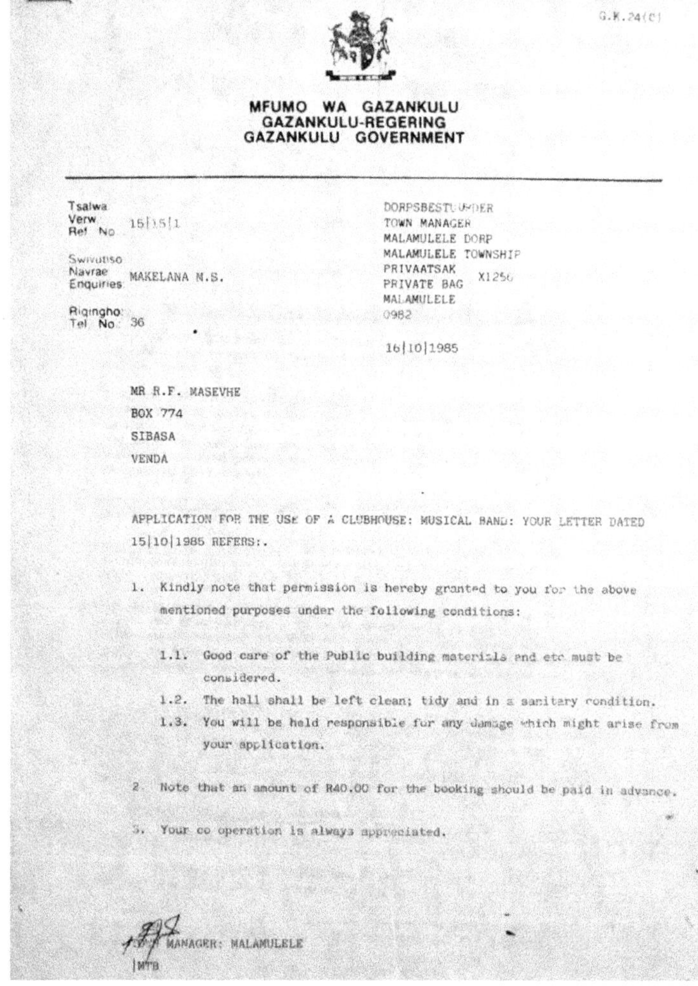

G.K.24(C)

**MFUMO WA GAZANKULU**
**GAZANKULU-REGERING**
**GAZANKULU GOVERNMENT**

Tsalwa
Verw.        15|15|1
Ref. No.

Swivutiso
Navrae       MAKELANA N.S.
Enquiries

Riqingho:
Tel. No.  36

DORPSBESTUURDER
TOWN MANAGER
MALAMULELE DORP
MALAMULELE TOWNSHIP
PRIVAATSAK        X1256
PRIVATE BAG
MALAMULELE
0982

16|10|1985

MR R.F. MASEVHE

BOX 774

SIBASA

VENDA

APPLICATION FOR THE USE OF A CLUBHOUSE: MUSICAL BAND: YOUR LETTER DATED
15|10|1985 REFERS:.

1. Kindly note that permission is hereby granted to you for the above
   mentioned purposes under the following conditions:

   1.1. Good care of the Public building materials and etc. must be
        considered.
   1.2. The hall shall be left clean; tidy and in a sanitary condition.
   1.3. You will be held responsible for any damage which might arise from
        your application.

2. Note that an amount of R40.00 for the booking should be paid in advance.

3. Your co operation is always appreciated.

TOWN MANAGER: MALAMULELE

|MTB

yet recorded.

# EXCELLENT RECORD

## LIST OF CRUSADES 1987

| DATE | PLACE | SECOND DATE (F) | VENUE |
|---|---|---|---|
| 4/12/87 | MUKULA | | MUKULA H: SCHOO |
| 5/12/87 | THOHOYANDOU | | VENDA SUN HOT |
| 06/12/87 | HA-MASHALBA — CANCELLED TO 24th Dece. | | .................... |
| 08/12/87 | DZT HIDI | | DEN.ga. TSHIVHA |
| 10/12/87 | HA-MASIA | | TSHIRUNZANANI |
| 11/12/87 | MAKONDE | | MAKO.NDE RESI: |
| 12/12/87 | NZHELELE/THONONDA | | THONONDA. SCHOO |
| 13/12/87 | SHAKADZA | | SHAKADZA SCHO |
| 16/12/87 | NGOVHELA | | NGOVHELA H/P.Sc |
| 18/12/87 | VLYFONTEIN | | Comm. HALL |
| 19/12/87 | HA-MASIA | | MASIA. H/P. SCHOO |
| 22/12/87 | | | :.................. |
| 23/12/87 | HA-KHAKHU MADOMBIDZA/HA-SINTHULULE | | KHAKHU H: SCHOOL MADOMBIDZHA. HAL |
| 24/12/87 | HA-MASHALIBA | | MASHAMBA H: SCHOO |
| 26/12/87 | THOHOYANDOU | | FESTIVAL |
| 28/12/87 | NIANI (TSHIKUNDAMALEMA | | TSHIPISE F: GROUND |
| 30/12/87 | HA-MULIMA | | FOOTBALL GROUND |
| 31/12/87 | MESSINA | | Comm: Holl |
| 1/01/88 | HA-SINTHULULE | | MADABANI |

WE WILL BE ABLE TO GO AND PERFORM IN ALL THOSE PLACES
IN GOD'S NAME WHO STRENGTHEN US.
IT IS TERMED "OPERATION CLEAR IT OUT"

## RESPONSE BY BISHOP ELIJAH MASWANGANYI
## TO INVITATION FROM BISHOP MASEVHE

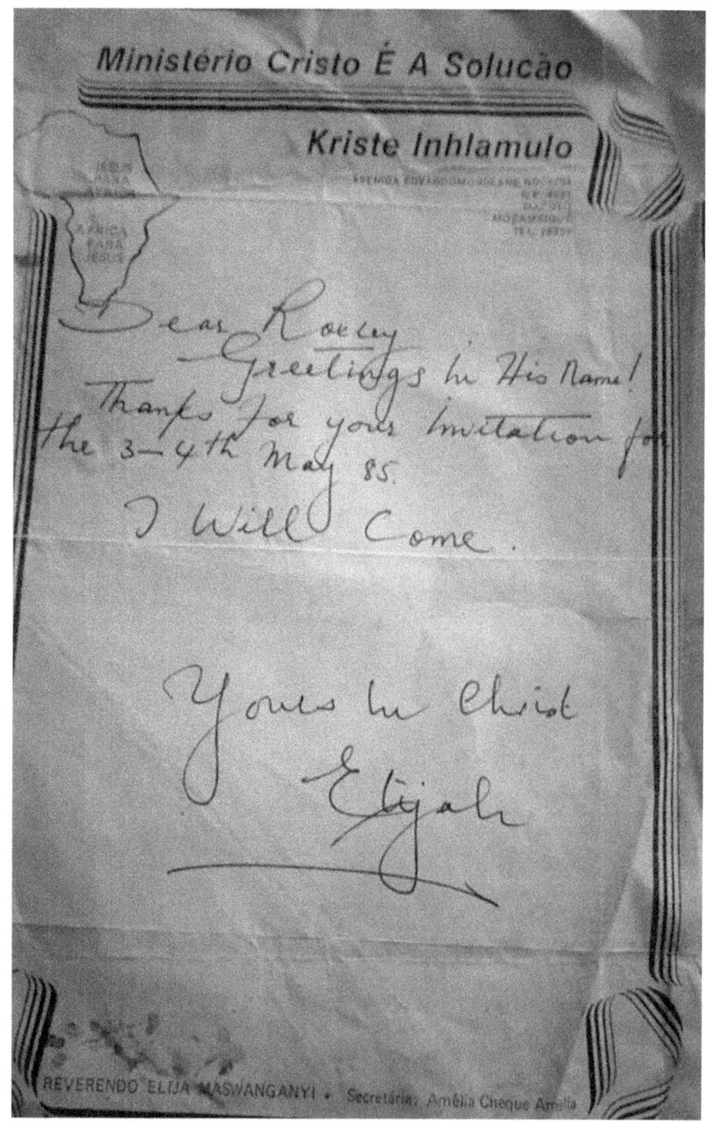

# THIRD NATIONAL SONG FESTIVAL

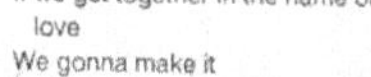


**Radio Venda**

## In the Name of Love

Record company:  Rea Music

Composer/Komponis

ROXLEY FHATUWANI
MASEVHE

For the second consecutive year, Roxley is the winner for Radio Venda. In 1959, at an early age, he started dancing to the rhythm of a boiling pot. He was a traditional dancing star, and played the drums for ancestor-worshipping ceremonies. He acquired his first guitar in 1978, and in the same year Radio Venda began to record his music. This was followed by several LP record releases, and in 1985 he won the Astera Award as the Top Soloist on record. His latest LP, "Lufuno (Love)", was released in 1986.

Roxley is vir die tweede agtereenvolgende jaar die wenner vir Radio Venda. Hy was van kleins af ritmies aangelê en sy gunsteling-tydverdryf was om op die maat van 'n kokende pot te dans. Hy het ook die tromme gespeel tydens voorvaderaanbiddingseremonies. Hy het in 1978 sy eerste ghitaar aangeskaf en in dieselfde jaar het Radio Venda opnames van sy musiek begin maak. Hy het al talle langspeelplate gemaak en in 1985 is hy beloon met 'n Astera-toekenning as die Beste Soloplatekunstenaar. Sy jongste langspeelplaat, "Lufuno (Liefde)", is in 1986 uitgereik.

If we get together in the name of love
We gonna make it
Let the whole world be
  baptised in the name of
  love, we can make it.
Love is the international anthem we
  all have to sing

Love is long suffering and kind
Love is not jealous, it does not brag
Love cannot kill, love cannot steal
Love bears all things, believes all
  things
Hopes all things and endures all
  things
If we speak in the tongues
  of men and angels
But do not have love
We have become a sounding
  brass or a clanging cymbal

You can move all the mountains
But if you do not have love
you are nothing
Love is stronger than death,
  It can do everything
Love cannot die, always alive
  and kicking
Let the whole world, in the
  name of love,
be in a love spree

**Chorus**
*In the name of love
  we can make it
Together in love
  we gonna make it
Lufuno lu na maanda /
  love has power
Lufuno la a kona /
  love can do it*

*Lufuno ndi mulalo /
  love is peace
Lufuno lu na maanda /
  love has power
Hooyi - he-he-he -
  Ahee h - hoo - ahee
hoo-ho - hoo - ahee -
  ahe-he - ahoo*

If we stand up in the name of
  love
Life shall be like a big party
Love can heal the cancer of
  hatred and enmity
Love can wipe all the tears
  and bring up billions of smiles
Love never fails, 'tis worth more
  than diamonds
Let's dream in the name of love
Our dream gonna come true
In this part of the world we need
  love
Let's be loving and lovely
Without love our future is gonna
  be gloomy, I say,
with love on our side we gonna
reap good fruits.

Love cannot sow the seed of
  confusion
Love can climb all the mountains,
It can cross all the seas
Love is never expensive, we can
  all practice with success.
If we get down in the name of love,
  we gonna reap success.
Let's declare the war of love
We gonna make things happen.

**Chorus**

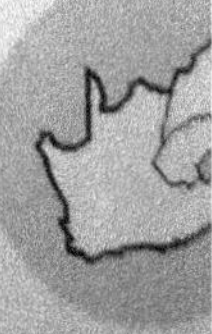

## PERFORMING AT STANDARD BANK ARENA

...ley Masevhe and his backing group in action at the Standard Bank Arena in last ...'s National Song Festival final.

## BISHOP MASEVHE AND HIS FRIEND PROFESSOR DOCTOR ṆEḒOHE

# KEEPER

Bishop Masevhe is also an excellent record keeper brain-wise and in practice.

He is honest enough though, to admit that due to age, his mind is not as sharp as it used to be but still, he remembers a lot of things that happened donkey years ago.

Below are some of the old records that he has kept safely, his memoirs. There is notably an anointing of a scribe in Bishop Masevhe.

# TO GOD BE ALL THE GLORY

Isaiah 43:19, KJV

*19 "Behold, I will do a new thing; now it shall spring forth; shall ye not know it? I will even make a way in the wilderness and rivers in the desert."*

# BIBLIOGRAPHY

Lostlake Music. (2020, February 02). Lostlake Music. Retrieved from APPRECIATING THE CONCERTINA: LEARNING THE BASICS OF PLAYING: http://lostlake-music.com/archives/45

The tribe. (2020, February 19). Facebook-wearethetribe1. Retrieved from Facebook-wearethetribe1: https://www.facebook.com/Wearethetribe1/posts/this-kalanga-super-food-is-super-good-for-your-health-there-is-a-very-good-reaso/825708504441086/

Wikipedia. (2020, June 26). Mbaqanga. Retrieved from From Wikipedia, the free encyclopedia: https://en.wikipedia.org/wiki/Mbaqanga

Wikipedia, t. f. (2020, JULY 14). Rock hyrax. Retrieved from Wikipedia, the free encyclopedia: https://en.wikipedia.org/wiki/Rock_hyrax

Wikipedia, t. f. (2020, June 28). University of South Africa. Retrieved from Wikipedia, the free encyclopedia: https://en.wikipedia.org/wiki/University_of_South_Africa

Wikipedia, the free encyclopedia. (2019, April 01). Plunge dip. Retrieved from Wikipedia, the free encyclopedia: https://en.wikipedia.org/wiki/Plunge_dip

# ABOUT THE AUTHOR

Ndivhuho Ṱhavhana is a duly admitted attorney, employed as a legal advisor in the public service in RSA.

She resides in Limpopo Province in South Africa. Her parents are Simeon and Ruthmary Ṱhavhana. She is the mother of four girls: Aluwani, Rudzani, Phaṱhutshedzo, and Thabelo.

She is a graphic designer with creative skills, amongst others: website building, video editing, audio editing, and ghost writing.

She is a Christian and fellowships at Kutama Pentecostal Holiness Church under Reverend Samuel Mametsa.

Other books she has published:

1) Ensnared (2011).

2) When bad things happen (2020).

3) The apple doesn't fall far from the tree (2020).

Facebook Name: Ndivhuho Gadisi Thavhana.

Cell: (+27 61 498 0872)

Email: **Ndivhuhot@gmail.com**

**Dr (Bishop) Roxley Fhatuwani  Masevhe- AUGUST 2020**